THE
LYING
APE

THE
LYING
APE

An Honest Guide to a World of Deception

Brian King

ICON BOOKS

Originally published in 2006 by Icon Books Ltd.

This edition published in the UK in 2007 by
Icon Books Ltd, The Old Dairy,
Brook Road, Thriplow,
Cambridge SG8 7RG
email: info@iconbooks.co.uk
www.iconbooks.co.uk

Sold in the UK, Europe, South Africa and Asia
by Faber & Faber Ltd, 3 Queen Square,
London WC1N 3AU
or their agents

Distributed in the UK, Europe, South Africa and Asia
by TBS Ltd, TBS Distribution Centre, Colchester Road
Frating Green, Colchester CO7 7DW

This edition published in Australia in 2007
by Allen & Unwin Pty Ltd,
PO Box 8500, 83 Alexander Street,
Crows Nest, NSW 2065

This edition published in the United States
in 2007 by Totem Books
Inquiries to Icon Books Ltd.,
The Old Dairy, Brook Road,
Thriplow, Cambridge
SG8 7RG, UK

Distributed to the trade in the USA by
National Book Network Inc.,
4501 Forbes Blvd, Suite 200
Lanham, Maryland 20706

Distributed in Canada by
Penguin Books Canada,
90 Eglinton Avenue East, Suite 700,
Toronto, Ontario M4P 2YE

ISBN 10: 1-84046-799-1
ISBN 13: 978-1840467-99-4

Typesetting by Hands Fotoset

Printed and bound in the UK by
Bookmarque

Contents

About the author

Brian King is an award-winning pioneer of radio fly-on-the-wall documentaries, the producer of hundreds of features, plays and comedy programmes for BBC Radio 4, and, with Martin Plimmer, the co-author of the bestselling *Beyond Coincidence* (Icon, 2004).

To Di. For believing in me.

Acknowledgements

In the interests of complete honesty, and as much as I would like to claim all the credit for myself, I have to admit that I couldn't have written this book without the generous help of a few people.

Particular thanks are due to my good and clever friends Martin Plimmer and Michael Magenis for pointing me in the direction of some great lies and for their general encouragement and advice; to my excellent editor Duncan Heath for his sage-like counsel and for keeping me off the path of purple prose; and to my wife, Di, for her unfailing support and unerring ability to spot my 'deliberate' mistakes.

Thanks also to the following for their invaluable contributions: broadcaster John Humphrys, psychological magician Derren Brown, solicitors Paul Drew and Michael Ive, publicist Mark (creative with the truth) Borkowski, psychiatrist Sean Spence, psychologists Martin Skinner, Darius Galasinski, Paul Ekman and Paul Seagar, insurance fraud investigator John Freeman, police instructor PC Steve Savell and broadcaster Dylan Winter (for the language of the car salesmen).

And I suppose I should thank each and every one of you out there for being such congenital and incorrigible liars, without whom this book would not have been necessary.

Foreword

Every word in this book is true. I may have accidentally arranged some of them into misleading sentences, but I hope not.

CHAPTER ONE

Problem, what problem?

Everybody lies – every day; every hour; awake; asleep; in his dreams; in his joy; in his mourning; if he keeps his tongue still, his hands, his feet, his eyes, his attitude, will convey deception.

Mark Twain

This book dismantles the most impenetrable of language barriers.

We're not talking about the language barrier that separates British tourists from almost everyone in the non-English-speaking world, nor that which exists between most thirteen-year-olds and the rest of humanity.

The language barrier we're concerned with here is far more pernicious. It's the barrier we erect between what we say and what we mean – between our lies and the plain, unadulterated truth.

Mendacity and deceit envelop and bedevil all our lives. We're told that our call is important, that our complaint is being dealt with urgently, that a second-hand car has been regularly serviced, that our pension fund is secure, that Botox will 'erase the effects of time', that our small bag of chips is actually 'regular fries' and that weapons of mass destruction can be launched against us in 45 minutes.

This book runs liars to ground and tears off their masks.

* * *

Lies are available in a whole range of colours. Black lies are the callous, greed-driven, destructive kind, designed to rob us of our money, our rights or even our lives. White lies reside at the other end of the scale and are far less damaging, though seldom entirely harmless. Then there are yellow lies, those told out of cowardice. When we exaggerate the size of the fish that got away, we tell a purple lie. Blue lies are told by the police. Government ministers who say they want to protect the environment are probably telling green lies. The vast majority of lies are casual, opportunistic, workaday deceptions – grey lies. Here's an example of a grey lie.

Back in the early 1970s I used to travel, as frequently as my meagre cub reporter's salary would allow, to Dublin – drawn by the twin attractions of the Guinness and an Irish nurse I'd met while busking in Amsterdam. During one visit, we drove up into the Wicklow Mountains in her aged Volkswagen Beetle; its broken accelerator linkages had been cunningly replaced by a piece of string trailing from the bonnet and through the driver's quarter-light. A series of deft tugs and jerks propelled us along our precarious way.

Travelling relentlessly upwards, we came upon establishments proudly displaying signs which read 'Paddy's Café. The highest café in Ireland', or 'McGinty's Bar. The highest pub in Ireland'. Nothing strange about that, except that as we continued towards the summit, other establishments hove into view, called 'O'Donnell's Café. The highest in Ireland', and

'O'Shaughnessy's. The highest pub in Ireland'. I'm making the names up, by the way; it was a long time ago.

On our way back down, we stopped for a drink in McGinty's Bar and asked how on earth they could claim to be the highest pub in Ireland when, patently, they were some several hundred feet closer to sea-level than O'Shaughnessy's or indeed the even more lofty Gerry's Bar, which all but straddled the summit and seemed to have an irresistible claim to the title. The explanation, we were soberly informed, was that the sign was designed specifically for travellers headed up the mountain. 'It's to let them know that we are the highest pub – *so far*', explained the unabashed publican.

This is certainly not the deadliest of deceptions – or indeed the loftiest of lies. It sits, perhaps, somewhere on the nursery slopes of a mountain of lies. By the way, the pub currently claiming to be the highest in Ireland is Johnny Fox's in Glencullen in the Dublin Mountains, which is, according to various tourism websites, 'allegedly' the highest pub in Ireland, or 'famed' as the highest pub in Ireland or 'reputed to be' the highest pub in Ireland. The pub's own website is less circumspect, and says it is 'one of Ireland's oldest and most famous pubs and *undoubtedly* the highest pub in the country'. I don't doubt it.

On reflection, 'mountain of lies' is probably the wrong metaphor. A mountain of lies would be conspicuous and easily manoeuvred around. In fact, we live at the heart of a jungle of lies. Falsehoods swing from every vine. Half-truths and fictions lurk menacingly in the undergrowth like venomous snakes, striking at the unwary.

Manufacturers, retailers and utility companies dismiss our complaints with obfuscation and weasel words. Insurance companies use impenetrable verbiage and small print to reject our claims. We buy products, a holiday or even a house, based on attractive but grossly misleading information. Fraudsters ensnare us with promises of easy money. Journalists tell us that Elvis is alive or that Freddie Starr ate someone's hamster. Politicians assure us that they will make our lives better, will cut (or at least not raise) taxes, and that they 'did not have sexual relations with *that* woman'. In our jungle of lies, truth is often strangled at birth.

But we shouldn't be too quick to point an admonishing finger at the deception and lies of others. It isn't just *them*, the usual suspects, it's *us* as well. This book is as much about the lies we tell as the lies we are told.

We lie to our friends and our colleagues, our husbands and wives. We are lied to by our parents and lie to our children in turn. We treat the truth with alarmingly little respect, finding it tiresome, inadequate or contrary to our interests; best avoided. In fact, we don't have to learn to lie – it comes naturally.

We lie to cover our mistakes and to exaggerate our achievements. We lie to flatter and ingratiate and amuse. We lie to avoid appearing stupid. We lie to win arguments and approval. We lie to avoid getting what we deserve. We lie to get someone into bed, or to conceal an affair. We lie to avoid paying tax, to line our pockets and to stay out of prison. We lie to be kind and we lie to be cruel. We lie often without compunction, and yet can be enraged if anyone dares to call us a liar.

So we shouldn't be remotely surprised by the deceitful behaviour of second-hand car salesmen, estate agents, advertisers, journalists and politicians. They are only using the natural skills and instincts we are all born with.

Yes, the unpalatable truth examined in this book is that all human beings are liars, albeit some are lesser-spotted and others great-crested varieties. It isn't, as the old cowboy films suggested, just the white man who speaks with forked tongue. We are all, irrespective or colour, class or creed, capable of being economical, indeed parsimonious with the truth. In fact, more than capable – skilled.

Our nakedness as a species is not, of course, the only feature that distinguishes us from other apes. Our disproportionately large brain, our self-awareness, our facility for speech and one other significant factor (a product of all of these) marks us out from the rest of the primates, indeed from all other animals – our ability to lie.

We are not, of course, the only life-form on the planet capable of acts of deception, but we are certainly the most adept and prolific. Our gift of language enables us to lie, literally, though our teeth – and we don't waste the opportunity. We speak, therefore we lie. We are *The Lying Ape*.

* * *

We take our unique aptitude for lying into every nook and cranny of our lives. Some lies are so commonly told, they become transparent.

Our cheque is in the post.

I'll start my diet tomorrow.

This is going to hurt me more than it hurts you.

Your table will be ready in a few minutes.

We can't deal with your complaint, our computer is down.

Let's have lunch sometime.

You haven't changed a bit.

I never got the message.

And, of course …

I love you.

Given the choice between confessing an uncomfortable truth or indulging in a little light dissembling, most of us, most of the time, will plump for the less scrupulously honest option. Lies provide us with a comfort zone – a buffer against the vicissitudes of life. A timely piece of mendacity might get us out of a tight spot, but it often places the pressure firmly on someone else.

Let's say, for example, you have a problem with your office computer. The technician whose job it is to fix it, can, if stumped, easily hide behind jargon. 'Your USB reboot web interface copulator is knackered, mate. Never known that to happen before. My supervisor can look at it when he comes in next Thursday week. Here's a pencil.'

Or he can go one better and avoid seeing you at all, as I discovered a few years ago while working on a BBC radio programme. Rushing to meet a deadline, I had just finished a script and was about to print it when, disaster, my computer completely gave up the ghost. I rang the IT support unit and begged for help.

> 'We'll be with you as soon as possible.'
> 'How long exactly?'
> 'About 30 minutes.'
> 'Can you get here any quicker? I really need to get my computer working as soon as possible.'

'We'll get there as soon as we can.'

Half an hour later, no technician in sight, I rang back to, politely, re-emphasise the urgency of the situation.

> 'Sorry, we'll be with you any minute now. We're very
>   busy at the moment.'
> 'Please hurry.'

Twenty minutes later. Still no technician. I reached for the phone. When, for heaven's sake (I don't think that was exactly the phrase I used), will he be here?

> 'He's leaving the office right now, just walking out the
>   door.'
> 'Thank you. Thank you. Thank you.'

Another fifteen minutes elapsed. I snatched up the phone.

> 'Where is he?'
> 'We're very busy at the moment.'
> 'I know, you told me. You also told me a quarter of an
>   hour ago that the technician was leaving the office on
>   his way to sort out my problem.'
> 'No, I said he was leaving the office. I didn't say he was
>   going to see you.'

You might think that a bit of a grey lie; but it seemed bible-black to me.

* * *

And lies can be dangerous things.

For every time she shouted 'fire!'
They only answered 'Little liar!'
And therefore when her Aunt returned,
Matilda, and the house, were burned.

Matilda's attention-seeking lies, like those of her famous predecessor, the little boy who cried 'wolf', proved fatal.

Fortunately, in the real world, the fire service will rush to your rescue however many times you shout 'fire!' Firemen in the UK turn out to around 30,000 malicious false alarms every year. That's 30,000 lying Matildas.

That, I suppose, is lying for kicks. In Japan they have been known to lie for food. For centuries fish was the nation's main source of protein, because Buddhist law forbade the consumption of any four-legged animal. But in 1872 the Japanese came up with a cunning little deception to get around the problem – they renamed wild boar 'mountain whale'. And today, in a ploy designed to win a lifting of the international ban on the country's profitable whaling industry, they describe even the magnificent and endangered blue whales as 'cockroaches of the sea'.

Not all lies are malicious or self-seeking, of course. Lies can be entertaining and fun – and lies can be kind. Lies oil the wheels of society, often keeping us from each other's throats. A world in which only the truth were spoken would be a strange and not particularly attractive place.

Lies play a much bigger part in our lives than most of us realise or care to acknowledge. We are enveloped in a creeping culture of deception from the cradle to the grave. And we can benefit from being both more aware of the lies we tell and more alert to the lies we are told.

CHAPTER TWO

The roots of deception

When my love swears that she is made of truth
I do believe her, though I know she lies,
That she might think me some untutor'd youth,
Unlearnèd in the world's false subtleties.
Thus vainly thinking that she thinks me young,
Although she knows my days are past the best,
Simply I credit her false-speaking tongue;
On both sides thus is simple truth suppress'd.
But wherefore says she not she is unjust,
And wherefore say not I that I am old?
O, love's best habit is in seeming trust,
And age in love loves not t'have years told.
    Therefore I lie with her, and she with me,
    And in our faults by lies we flattered be.

Shakespeare, Sonnet 138

Lying is as natural to us as breathing. Telling the truth is the difficult thing. Those who claim they never tell lies are deluded – or lying. Lies are at the heart of almost all human interaction and we've been telling them since the dawn of civilisation.

Lies can be big and beastly, and we'll come to those later.

Deception begins at home – and you don't even have to get out of bed.

In a survey of 5,000 women, a staggering (from a male perspective) 46 per cent admitted that they either did fake, or had faked, orgasms. *That's Life* magazine reveals they mostly did it to 'spare my partner's feelings', or because 'I didn't want to emasculate him'. But they were still lying. The earth hadn't moved for them.

George Washington, we're told, didn't do it, and nor did Superman. Lie that is, not fake orgasms. The rest of us lie to each other on a regular basis. And there's plenty of evidence to prove it.

American psychologist Bella DePaulo conducted a series of studies involving students and members of the public, inviting them to record details of all the lies they told during social interactions lasting more than ten minutes. She discovered that, on average, people lied a fraction under two times a day – and in a quarter of all social encounters. The students reported that they lied frequently to their mothers, often for financial reasons. One lied about the price she had to pay for a typewriter so that her parents would send her more money. Others lied to hide the fact that they were smoking or drinking. Overall, the participants didn't feel particularly uncomfortable about lying and believed their lies were detected in only 18 per cent of cases.

But it's quite likely that many of the participants under-estimated the extent of their own lying behaviour, failing to recognise small deceptions involving exaggeration, evasion and other minor deviations from the truth. And choosing not to count lies told during social interactions of less than ten minutes seems unnecessarily proscriptive. A variety of scientific and not-so-scientific studies in Britain seem to settle on an average figure of around six lies a day – which sounds more like it to me. One Gallup poll put the figure at twenty lies a day. This is not an exact science.

The *That's Life* survey in 2004 concluded that 96 per cent of British women routinely tell lies. Half of the 5,000 women interviewed admitted telling little white lies most days, but eight out of ten also owned up to occasional 'big life-changing lies' as well. Half of all women would lie to their husbands or partners if the baby they were carrying was not his, and four in ten women would lie about contraception to get pregnant. 'Modern women just can't stop lying, but they do it to stop hurting other people's feelings', says the magazine's editor. And to manipulate the men in their lives, obviously.

Men, of course, can hold their own in the lying stakes, particularly where adultery is concerned. Samuel Pepys set the standard back in November 1668, covering up his infidelity with his maid Deb:

> Up, and I did, by a little note which I flung to Deb, advise her that I did deny that I ever kissed her, and so she might govern herself. The truth [is] that I did adventure upon God's pardoning me this lie, knowing how heavy a thing it would be for me to be the ruin of the poor girl; and next, knowing that if my wife should know all, it were impossible ever for her to be at peace with me again.

Though the deception of an adulterous spouse, when exposed, may drive a couple apart, few relationships would last long without lies. Honesty can be cruel and as hard to forgive as deception; harder sometimes.

Writer Penny Vincenzi recommends lying. Her 1977 book *Compleat Liar* advises those caught in the act of adultery not, under any circumstances, to tell the truth. She doesn't attempt to defend or excuse adultery, but suggests it can be made less painful by the application of a few well-selected lies. There's nothing to be gained, she argues, by one partner saying to another: 'I want to tell you that I've slept with Fred/Doris and it was most enjoyable.' And if caught in the act, she recommends:

> Say it was the very first time; say you were doing it because he or she had promised you a rise, or a cheap mortgage or a course of free driving lessons. Say that he (or she) was a sex therapist and you were seeking to improve your technique (and thence your marriage). Say you didn't want to; say you couldn't help it; say you can't remember how you got there. Say anything at all, so long as it's a lie.

Vincenzi also suggests that the adulterer should keep his or her lies elaborate because that makes them harder to disprove. I've always thought the general rule was that lies should be kept simple so they can be better remembered. Either way, bear in mind the cautionary words of Sir Walter Scott: 'O what a tangled web we weave, / When first we practise to deceive!' These kind of lies, once spawned, can beget wriggling infant lies, which themselves sprout grotesque offspring, as writer Martin Plimmer illuminates in his mini-drama, 'The Lying Cad'.

> 'That Team Conference', he says, 'I thought it would never end!'
> She replies: 'I thought Team Conference was Thursday.'
> 'They brought it forward this week.'
> 'Well at least you'll be home early on Thursday.'
> 'No … there's an extra one on Thursday.'
> 'Why?'
> 'To … to discuss the Dutch project.'

'Tony's wife told me the Dutch project was cancelled.'
'Cancelled? Of course not!'
'But Tony's binned all his demonstration Edams. We
      must go round there immediately and warn him!'

And so on, he warns, until hand-to-hand fighting is the only
option.

Go to work on a lie

Circumlocution of the truth is as common in the workplace as
it is in the home. We arrive late at the office because, after a
night out on the tiles, we overslept. We tell our employer that
our train was delayed, our child was sick or the dog swallowed
the alarm clock. More imaginative liars will regale the boss
with tales of resuscitating a heart attack victim, or saving a
drowning infant from a canal. The latter excuse tends to work
particularly well if you arrive in the office dripping wet. If we
need a day off to see the cricket or for a day at the races, our
grandmother has to be buried (again), or we go down with 24-
hour flu or a sudden attack of ingrowing toenail.

Then there's the man who tells his boss that he was absent
on Cup Final day because he had to take his mother to the
hospital. 'That's strange', says the boss. 'The same thing
happened during the Test Match, on Grand National day and
during Wimbledon.' 'My God', says the man. 'You don't think
she's faking it, do you?'

Incidentally, a survey of office workers established that the
British are the most prolific liars in Europe. Eleven per cent of
Britons admitted they would deny having received an e-mail in
order to excuse their failure to respond to it. This compared
with 4 per cent of Spanish workers, 3 per cent of French and
Italians, and just 1 per cent of Germans.

* * *

We find it remarkably difficult to leave the truth unadorned. We want to appear better than our natural talents allow. We don't like to accept blame, to acknowledge our fallibility, to admit we're wrong or to say sorry. So we generate a force-field of fiction to protect ourselves from the dull, inconvenient or unacceptable truth.

Lies sometimes slip out before we can stop them, particularly when we're being drawn out of our depth.

HIM: So it's blindingly obvious that the existence of a person comes chronologically before his or her essence. Don't you agree?

YOU: Oh yes. Definitely.

HIM: You've read Sartre on the subject, I take it?

YOU (LYING): Of course.

HIM: So what did you make of *Existentialism is a Humanism*?

YOU: Oh … um … interesting. The ending was a bit sad, though.

HIM (AFTER PAUSE): You've not actually read Sartre, have you?

YOU: Are you talking about Jean-Paul Sartre?

HIM: Yes, of course.

YOU: Oh, I see. I thought you meant Daphne Sartre, who wrote the existentialist pop-up book for children.

HIM: An easy mistake to make.

YOU (THINKS): Phew. Nearly made a fool of myself there.

And who has ever filled in a road accident claim form without applying a little creativity; perhaps knocking 15 miles per hour off their speed, claiming their faulty brake lights were functioning perfectly or that they had indicated right when in fact they had indicated left? Some people, worried that an outright lie will get them into deeper trouble, resort to contortions of the truth. This can produce farcical results, as comedian Jasper Carrott discovered when looking through a collection of genuine claim forms submitted to a major insurance company. Among the gems he discovered:

> 'The accident was due to an invisible lorry narrowly missing me.'
> 'I bumped into a stationary tree coming in the other direction.'
> 'The other man altered his mind and I had to run over him.'
> 'A pedestrian hit me and went under my car.'
> 'The guy was all over the road. I had to swerve a number of times before I hit him.'
> 'I knocked over a man. He admitted it was his fault as he had been knocked down before.'

In August 2005, a Cheshire couple went to extraordinary lengths to avoid paying a couple of £60 speeding tickets. Stewart and Cathryn Bromley embarked on an elaborate deception after their Mercedes was caught twice by a speed camera close to their home in Manchester. They attempted to convince the police that an imaginary former work colleague from Bulgaria had borrowed their car at the time. When police became suspicious, Mrs Bromley flew to Bulgaria and sent a postcard purporting to be from a Konstantin Koscov. It read:

> Many thanks for the opportunity to work in your office. I enjoyed the experience and would gladly return the favour. Unfortunately my car is nowhere near as

good as yours but it will get you about! Many thanks again and look forward to my next trip. Regards, Konstantin Koscov.

But the police found the coincidence too hard to swallow, and a few simple inquiries quickly established that no such person existed. The Bromleys eventually pleaded guilty to two charges of perverting the course of justice and were fined over £9,000.

Again we see how relatively minor deceptions can rapidly balloon out of control. Lies are volatile and seductive things. Modest expenses-fiddling, for example, can so easily develop into major fraud. But that's another chapter.

For further evidence of our capacity to deviate imaginatively from the truth, take a look at the personal ads placed in newspapers and magazines by lonely souls looking for a little love and affection. This is a fantasy world in which large ladies become 'voluptuous' and seven-stone weaklings transmogrify into 'wiry'. Alcoholics are 'amiable' and a 'laid-back male' is, in reality, a chronically shy introvert. It's an environment in which everyone is attractive, single, footloose, fancy-free and in possession of a GSOH.

Lies are also useful for avoiding confrontation and are deployed in even the least threatening of situations. In a restaurant, for example, we will spend half an hour complaining amongst ourselves that the service is too slow, the food is cold, the meat overcooked and the vegetables taste of nothing. Then the waiter approaches and asks if everything is OK.

'Fine', we say. 'Great, thanks.'
'Sure?'
'Absolutely.'

Psychologist Darius Galasinski grew up in Poland but now works at the University of Wolverhampton. He's fascinated by what he sees as a rather strange British obsession with the phrase *I'm fine*. 'When people say it they are nearly always lying', he says. 'I say *how are you?* and they say *I'm fine*. Everyone is always fine. Sometimes when they ask me how I am, I say *frustrated* and they reply *I'm fine too*.'

The first liar

When, as a species, did we first enter this twilight zone of half-truths, invention and outright mendacity? Is it a relatively recent phenomenon, a consequence of modern civilisation with its pressures to succeed and its social imperatives – or has it always been like this? Who were the first liars? What was the very first lie?

Oscar Wilde believed the world's first liar was 'he who first, without having gone out to the rude chase, told the wandering cavemen at sunset how he had slain the Mammoth in single combat.'

Wilde is probably about right with his timing. In order to lie effectively, we need words. No one knows precisely when the first words were spoken. Stephen Pinker, author of *The Language Instinct*, assumes that language, like other instincts, evolved by natural selection and may have begun as far back as 2.5 million years ago with *Homo habilis*, whose stone tools suggested 'a degree of cooperation and acquired technology'.

Language obviously helped our prehistoric ancestors to master their environment, hunt more effectively and defeat their enemies. But it's quite likely that it was also used less altruistically; that this was also about the time that *Homo deceptus* first stalked the Earth. Given the eventual direction of human development, it's probable that the language of deception would have evolved pretty much simultaneously with the language of communication, or at least very soon after. The most successful *Homo sapiens* may have been those who most quickly learned how to use language to advance their personal agendas. Survival of the fittest liar.

How useful to have language at your disposal to trick a rival into entering the sabre-toothed tiger's lair, or to woo the most desirable mate with false promises and idle flattery and, a little later perhaps, to exaggerate the reliability of a second-hand wheel, or the safety features of fire, or to extol the dubious virtues of a damp and flea-infested semi-detached cave (with plenty of scope for improvement).

Evidence that the ability to lie probably developed very early in human evolution has been uncovered by ape-watchers who have detected deliberate and conscious deceptive behaviour among our closest animal relatives.

Most famously, the San Francisco Zoo gorilla, Koko, who has been taught sign language, is reported to have ripped out a steel sink unit and then signed 'cat did it', pointing to its tiny pet kitten. Koko's keepers, however, admit they aren't sure if the gorilla was deliberately lying or just joking.

But primatologists Richard Byrne and Nadia Corp, from St Andrews University, discovered that certain monkeys and apes are perfectly capable of deceiving each other for personal gain. A female gorilla, for example, will mate with a male surreptitiously to avoid a beating from a more dominant male. And monkeys will feign lack of interest in tasty food so that others don't come and steal it.

Byrne observed a young baboon avoiding a reprimand from its mother by suddenly standing to attention and scanning the horizon, fooling the entire troop into panicking about a possible rival group nearby. He was rather shocked that baboons could do anything quite as subtle as that.

The frequency of deception in a species turns out to be in direct proportion to the size of the animal's neocortex. Bush babies and lemurs, which have a relatively small neocortex, were among the least sneaky. The most 'tactically deceptive' primates included macaques and the great apes – gorillas, chimpanzees, bonobos and orang-utans – all of which are endowed with a large neocortex. So the brainier the ape, the more deceptive its behaviour. And who are the brainiest of all the apes? We are. The Lying Ape.

Inside the brain of the liar

At Sheffield University, psychiatrist Dr Sean Spence uses a room-sized electromagnet scanner to try to track down lies to their source – deep inside the brain. He puts people inside the machine, asks them to lie to him, and photographs their brains in the very act of deception. He might ask them what they ate for breakfast and they, having in reality enjoyed a bowl of cornflakes, reply 'porridge'. The MRI scanner, taking a picture every second, catches the lie as it wriggles into chemical and electrical life.

Inside his lie-laboratory, Dr Spence showed me brain-scan images revealing which areas of the brain became more active when the subject told lies, as opposed to the truth. The first were areas at the front of the brain, either side of the forehead (for the more technically-minded, the ventral-lateral prefrontal cortex), which mainly deal with inhibiting responses to the environment. Other areas towards the mid-line of the prefrontal region (think of the middle of your forehead, two centimetres behind your eyes) also become highly active. These are complex parts of the brain, principally concerned with controlling output, but which also monitor responses to the world.

From this evidence Dr Spence has established that, when we lie, the brain does two things.

1) It inhibits the truthful response.
2) It replaces the truthful response with something else – the lie.

He concludes that the urge to tell the truth is the 'primary force' or base-line – a guiding force that has to be resisted. The brain scans reveal that we have a basic instinct to tell the truth, but that we also have an equally natural facility to resist that instinct – to tell lies.

Dr Spence believes that the ability to choose between telling the truth and lying develops in early childhood; that we learn to lie as we learn to speak.

Out of the mouths of babes

A natural, instinctive facility to lie might, theoretically anyway, lie dormant. Those saintly people who resort to deception only on very special occasions probably have a very strong truthful primary force which overpowers their capacity for deceit. Or perhaps their parents administered high-voltage electric shocks whenever, as youngsters, they told a fib. The truth is that most children can lie their little heads off.

To be guilty of a lie, we must have what is described by scientists as a 'theory of mind', the ability to understand that other people have different thoughts to our own – and that they can be deceived. This is thought to develop around the age of three, alongside language skills. Once we have grasped this, there's no stopping us.

In an American study, a group of three-year-old children were left in a room and instructed not to turn around and look at a particular toy. When the experimenter came back after five minutes, she asked each child, 'Did you peek?' Although video recordings show that 90 per cent of the children did look, only 38 per cent told the truth and admitted it. A similar experiment involving children of various ages showed that the older the children were, the more likely they were to lie. By the age of five, none of the children would admit that they had looked at the toy.

Children are both natural and talented liars. This is certainly the view of psychologist Aldert Vrij from the University of Portsmouth. He offers the example of a three-year-old girl who responds with great enthusiasm when she receives a present from her grandmother, although in fact she does not like the present. 'Children are encouraged by their parents to tell these type of lies', he says.

Every parent is familiar with the frustrations of trying to get a small child to confess to a minor misdemeanour. We have a range of threats up our sleeve – to withdraw our love, to cancel an expensive (and already paid for) excursion, to never speak to the little darlings again, and, classically, to warn that Father Christmas doesn't bring presents for naughty boys and girls. When, inevitably, none of these threatened punishments materialises, the signal to the junior miscreant is clear – Mummy and Daddy don't always mean what they say. If they can lie, so can I.

And we provide the signals which motivate children to lie to avoid punishment. Vrij explains:

A two-year-old girl is told not to eat a biscuit. Later her mother asks the girl if she ate the biscuit. She admits it and the mother gets angry and punishes her. After this happens a few times, the child learns that admitting wrongdoing leads to punishment – therefore she starts to lie to avoid punishment. Then she learns that some of her lies are detected. Her parents tell her that it is bad to lie and that she will be punished if she lies. Now the child faces a dilemma. If she tells the truth about her wrongdoing she will be punished and if she lies she will be punished. Soon she learns that her parents do not detect all of her wrongdoing. It is therefore better for her to lie about her wrongdoing and to admit such behaviour only when she is detected.

Was this at least partly what Philip Larkin had in mind when he wrote:

> They fuck you up, your mum and dad.
> They may not mean to, but they do.
> They fill you with the faults they had
> And add some extra, just for you.

We bombard our children with lies; lies about tooth fairies and Santa Claus and bogeymen who lurk in the woods. Later we warn that thumb-sucking will cause warts, and we tell our sons that a certain activity will make them go blind. Is it really any wonder that they develop their own facility to lie and dissemble, and that they grow up to become estate agents, second-hand car salesmen and politicians? We are all Frankensteins, creating little monsters who find it all too easy to discard the truth.

Honing the skills of deception

So much for little liars. By the time we reach puberty, we have generally evolved into fairly sophisticated dissemblers. By early teens, proficiency at lying becomes a survival skill. We become impervious to guidance from adults on matters of truth and start to make our own rules. By our late teens, we have usually become spectacularly good liars.

On the day I went to see social psychologist Dr Martin

Skinner in his office at the University of Warwick, he had, by chance, spent much of the morning listening to a string of excuses from students who had failed to deliver important essays on time and wanted extensions.

'They've given me a variety of excuses involving bereavement, illness and IT failure', said Dr Skinner. 'Some of the excuses are quite elaborate – a portfolio of mini excuses. I'm more likely to believe a person who comes along with one vivid excuse, that the dog ate the essay for example, than the more contorted and detailed variety.'

Either way, his students tend to get what they want. 'It's hard not to give extensions without bringing in solicitors and searching for forensic evidence', he explained. 'I have to rely on their honesty.'

Martin Skinner understands why lying is important to human beings. Lies, he says, help to oil the wheels of social intercourse. As we acquire language and develop an 'interior life', we learn to dissemble, flatter and ingratiate, but also to work within the rules of lying. The truth hurts – so we respond to questions like 'Do I look fat in this?' or 'Do you love me?' with little white lies.

White lies are important because they enable us to maintain a sense of self-esteem. 'Self-esteem acts as a buffer against our terrible anxieties about life – and death', explains Dr Skinner. 'Feeling positive about ourselves protects us against those anxieties. When we are young, our parents surround us with unconditional positive regard, telling us we are clever and beautiful even if we aren't, and we develop that sense of worth. Much of the rest of our lives is spent maintaining our belief in ourselves – trading in images of self-worth.'

While these white lies have the power to make our lives more agreeable, they can also result in self-delusion and disappointment. Just watch an episode of one of those TV talent shows, *Pop Idol* or *The X-Factor*, where aspiring pop singers strut their stuff in front of a panel of judges. One typically untalented *X-Factor* hopeful performed a few tuneless bars of a Britney Spears number before being stopped and bluntly informed that she was murdering the song and was completely untalented. 'Give me a chance', she pleaded. 'I can sing. I can do it.' Outside the audition room, in tears, she complained that the judges had been unfair and had failed to recognise her talent. Undaunted, she set off to compete in the Miss Birmingham beauty competition, where, apparently, she failed to progress beyond the first round. This young girl was the innocent victim of deception; well-intentioned lies told to her all her short life, by parents and friends, that she was beautiful and talented. She had made the simple mistake of believing them.

Some people don't need the collusion of parents and friends to encourage them to go to extraordinary lengths to present themselves in a flattering light. 'Some of us want more than just bit parts in the self-esteem landscape', says Dr Skinner. 'We want to be stars. So we exaggerate our worth, or achievements, or what we know.' We'll be coming to Jeffrey Archer later.

Not all of our lies are to do with bolstering our own or each other's sense of self-worth, of course. Lies are just as likely to be told in the interests of greed, ambition and spite. So what, in the opinion of Dr Skinner, is the bottom line. Why do we lie?

'The answer to why we lie is because we can. It's all part of being human. The acid test of human consciousness is that we can lie. Self-consciousness and the ability to lie develop hand in hand. They are different aspects of the same process. People naturally lie and get other people to lie for them. It's all very destructive and depressing. There is an upside to being self-conscious, to being human – but this is a downside.'

Let's move rapidly on.

A short history of lying

This book is mainly concerned with the contemporary world of lies, but we should acknowledge that modern liars follow in an ignoble but impressive tradition of deceit, going back to at least the 4th century BC, when the Greek philosopher Diogenes conducted his futile search for a completely honest man.

The apostle Peter, the fisher of men, cast himself as a contender for the title of greatest liar of all time, with his thrice denial of Christ. Not that Jesus had ever believed his earlier protestations that he would 'rather die than betray my lord'.

But should we believe anything in the Bible? George Bernard Shaw's father taught him as a child that the Bible was the 'damndest parcel of lies ever invented'. George Bernard himself believed that the Bible contains 'a good many lies which ought never to be told to children'. He wrote: 'What civilization could any State build on these savage superstitions of vindictive theism and blood sacrifice? And who would now be obsessed by them if they had not been inculcated during infancy?'

The literal truth of the Bible was brought into question more recently after an American radio talk show host warned that homosexuality was an abomination according to Leviticus 18:22 and could not be condoned under any circumstances. The following is from a satirical response posted on the internet.

I have a neighbour who insists on working on the Sabbath. Exodus 35:2 clearly states he should be put to death. Am I morally obligated to kill him myself?

My uncle has a farm. He violates Leviticus 19:19 by planting two different crops in the same field, as does his wife by wearing garments made of two different kinds of thread (cotton/polyester blend). He also tends to curse and blaspheme a lot. Is it really necessary that we go to all the trouble of getting the whole town together to stone them? (Leviticus 24:10–16) Couldn't we just burn them to death at a private family affair, as we do with people who sleep with their in-laws? (Leviticus 20:14)

There have been many literary liars down the ages, but few compare with Sir John Mandeville, whose hugely popular 14th-century book – the *Travels of Sir John Mandeville* – led philosopher Thomas Browne to describe him as 'the greatest liar of all time'. This short but typical extract, describing the Indian Ocean islands of Andaman, gives you a good idea why:

> There are a great many different kinds of people in these isles. In one, there is a race of great stature, like giants, foul and horrible to look at; they have one eye only, in the middle of their foreheads. They eat raw flesh and raw fish. In another part, there are ugly folk without heads, who have eyes in each shoulder; their mouths are round, like a horseshoe, in the middle of their chest … In another isle there are ugly fellows whose upper lip is so big that when they sleep in the sun they cover all their faces with it. In another there are people of small stature, like dwarfs, a little bigger than pygmies. They have no mouth, but instead a little hole, and so when they must eat they suck their food through a reed or a pipe.

Christopher Columbus's great discoveries would not have been possible but for a bit of judicious deception. When he first set sail in search of a western route to the East Indies in 1492, he knew that his crew felt uneasy about travelling into unknown waters, so he kept two logs for the journey. In the first, he recorded the distances travelled as he calculated them. In the second log, he deliberately entered shorter distances so that his crew would think they were closer to home than they actually were. The men fell for it. Ironically, as it turned out, the phoney mileage figures were more accurate than his 'real' calculations.

Another 'greatest liar' contender is Titus Oates, the Anglican priest who fabricated the Popish Plot of 1678. A serial liar, he had been imprisoned for perjury while serving as a curate in Hastings in 1674. Four years later, Oates falsely claimed that there was a vast Jesuit conspiracy to assassinate Charles II and place his Roman Catholic brother, James, on the throne. News of the plot caused terror throughout London, and led to the executions of 35 innocent people. Charles himself had never been entirely convinced by Oates's story, but after James came to the throne, the priest was convicted of perjury and was pilloried, flogged, and imprisoned. He died in obscurity.

Some great liars need great fools to help them achieve their deception. There was no record of any survivors when the ship carrying Roger Tichborne, the son of a wealthy Hampshire family, went down in high seas in 1854. But his distraught mother would not accept that he was dead, and advertised around the world for news of him. The man who eventually turned up, claiming to be her son, was nothing like the skinny, foppish, French-speaking Tichborne. He was shorter, coarser, weighed 26 stone and seemed to have forgotten how to speak French. Nevertheless, the desperate and, frankly, barking mad Lady Tichborne accepted him as her son.

After she died, the family spent a fortune on a marathon court case which eventually ruled that the man, now identified as Arthur Orton from the East End of London, was indeed an impostor. He had embarked on his deception by reading about the family from Burke's *Peerage* and enhancing his knowledge with details gleaned from family members. He was subsequently convicted of perjury and jailed for fourteen years.

A more recent impostor was Anna Anderson, the woman

who insisted for decades, on television chat shows around the world, that she was Anastasia, the daughter of Czar Nicholas II, and had miraculously survived the Bolshevik massacre of the rest of her family. After her death, DNA tests proved her a liar.

The Piltdown Man hoax is one of the most extraordinary scientific frauds of all time. Between 1910 and 1912, Charles Dawson, an English lawyer and amateur geologist, found what appeared to be the fossilised fragments of a cranium, a jaw-bone, and other apparently human remains in gravel deposits at Barkham Manor, on Piltdown Common near Lewes in Sussex. These were identified by palaeontologists as belonging to a previously unknown species of hominid – the missing evolutionary link between apes and early humans. It wasn't until 1954 that the remains were properly identified as the skilfully disguised fragments of a modern human cranium, the jaw and teeth of an orang-utan, and the tooth of a chimpanzee. It has been widely assumed that the fraud was perpetrated by Dawson, possibly to win entrance to the Royal Society, but his guilt has never been proved.

One of the most audacious liars in recent history, and a personal favourite, was Brian Mackinnon, the 32-year-old Scot who, in 1993, posed as seventeen-year-old Canadian Brandon Lee to gain admission to Bearsden Academy in Glasgow in order to re-sit his A-levels. He wanted to qualify for medical school. What kind of convoluted lies must he have had to tell to keep his secret from his tutors and school-mates for two years? They were, by all accounts, suspicious, but could never quite manage to catch him out.

Just a few of the great liars in history, all behaving as nature intended. But then again, perhaps they were actually bad liars. If they had been good liars, we wouldn't know about them. The truly great liars, of course, are never detected. Look around. They're behind you.

CHAPTER THREE

Deviating from the truth

Two elderly women fall into conversation in a café:

ETHEL: I lost my husband, Bert, nearly twenty years ago.
DORIS: How was he taken?
ETHEL: His heart. Sudden. Didn't know what hit him.
DORIS: My husband passed away just six months ago.
ETHEL: Oh dear, What was it?
DORIS (DROPPING VOICE): It was ... it was the Big C.
ETHEL: Really. He drowned?

Clearly neither Ethel nor Doris is saying precisely what she means. Both women are tip-toeing around words they find disturbing, falling back on euphemisms. Ethel didn't lose her husband. He died. And Doris doesn't really want to know how he was *taken* (by hearse presumably); she wants to know *how* he died. But at least up to this point these women understand each other. The confusion sets in only when the euphemism becomes less familiar, at least to Ethel. Our two widows are not trying to deceive each other, but Ethel has, nevertheless, ended up being misled. The truth, in a real sense, has been lost.

Euphemisms, as we shall see, can be and are used to deliberately conceal meaning. More typically, however, they simply help to cushion us from the coarse and brutal realities of life (and death) as well as some of its more embarrassing moments. Usually they are barely lies at all, more like detours from the truth, and are mostly unselfish and well-meaning.

But even these mildest of linguistic deviations are not harmless. Their intention may be kind, but they add to the general web of confusion and misunderstanding surrounding us. We should categorise them as yellow or cowardly lies, as they often represent a failure of courage to speak the unpalatable truth.

Euphemism is a close linguistic cousin of those other forms of circumlocutory language, formal politeness, political correctness and, as it's known in common parlance, bullshit. But we'll come to those in a bit.

* * *

The English language, courtesy of words donated by Britain's various invaders over the centuries, provides us with a rich variety of ways to say more or less the same thing. You might, for example, find this book a regal (Latin), royal (French) or kingly (Anglo-Saxon) feast of ideas and information. Similarly, there are plenty of words available to describe more sensitive matters, like death or sex or the many other things which shock, embarrass or upset us. But, though spoiled for choice, we still frequently reject obvious or straightforward thesaurus-based options in favour of euphemism.

Much euphemism is of the 'passed away' or 'kicked the bucket' variety, which is neither intended to, nor succeeds, in deceiving. The meaning is widely understood, but the impact of the words has been softened. Not much harm has been done in our Ethel/Doris scenario. A moment's confusion perhaps, but Doris will eventually find a way of explaining the cause of her husband's sad demise without using the taboo word 'cancer'.

And euphemism can enrich language; as in the elegant phraseology of courtroom lawyers for example, designed to destroy the credibility of a witness without breaching the rules of court; or the circumlocutions of politicians, whose ability to hurl insults at opponents without contravening parliamentary etiquette we'll also look at a little later.

Euphemism can be gentle and funny. The actor John Le Mesurier left instructions when he died for his wife Joan to place a notice in *The Times* announcing that he had 'conked out'. It was his style. Seventeen years earlier, he had asked Joan to marry him, saying: 'I don't suppose you would take me on.' Joan says she wasn't quite sure if she had, in fact, been proposed to. There's a wonderful fictional example in the spoof rock documentary film *Spinal Tap*, in which the group's manager, when asked why the band are playing smaller and smaller venues, explains that they are not getting less popular, just 'more selective in their appeal'.

In December 1891, Miss Daisy Hopkins, a known prostitute, was arrested by officials of the University of Cambridge and charged with 'walking with a member of the University'. In polite academic circles, this was quite clearly understood to mean immoral behaviour. She was found guilty by the university court and ordered to be detained for fourteen days in the university gaol. But her lawyers succeeded in having the conviction quashed after convincing a High Court judge that 'walking' with someone was not anything that could be construed as an offence. In the face of a literal-minded judge, the euphemism employed by the Cambridge dons had backfired on them.

But euphemism, in clever but unprincipled hands, can be deeply and intentionally deceptive.

At the tail end of 2003, American mobile phone company Kyocera had a big problem with its model 7135 Smartphone. The batteries started overheating and exploding. It happened four times. In one instance, a Philadelphia man received second-degree burns to his leg. How could the company gently break the news to the 40,000 customers who had bought the model? They had a brainwave, and sent out letters to every customer warning that the batteries in their mobile phone might be prone to 'rapid disassembly'.

The story was reported in the *New Scientist*, where it was read by aerospace engineer Chris Elliot who, in turn, was prompted to write to the magazine with a confession. His job occasionally required him to produce what are known in the industry as 'failure mode effect analysis reports' which list potential product hazards. Certain words, he said, were expressly forbidden. 'Fire' had to be referred to as 'an uncontrolled thermal event', an explosion (as in Kyocera-land) as a 'spontaneous rapid disassembly event'; 'bursting' is an 'unplanned loss of containment', and 'crash' becomes 'deconstructive deceleration'. There is nothing gentle or kindly about such language. It is designed to achieve damage limitation, and used to disguise the truth.

Euphemism can take us down some tortuous linguistic highways and byways, contributing significantly to that language barrier which separates what we say from what we truly mean. In its most extreme form, euphemism can be deployed to hide or disguise the ugly realities of crime, war, and even – as in the case of 'ethnic cleansing' or 'the final solution' – genocide. For the moment, though, we're concerned with the way in which euphemism is used to skirt around the truth, rather than to turn it completely on its head.

What makes us do it? The publisher Jeremy Lewis felt that humankind wasn't able to bear too much reality. He wrote:

'Only the most robust can survive on a diet of raw truths and untenderised plain talking. Awkward customers who insist on calling a spade a spade can only be taken in small doses: kindliness and cowardice ensure that, for the rest of us, a mealymouthed reticence prevails.'

The Victorians were masters of mealy-mouthed reticence. They were famously inclined to replace the titillating word *leg* with the less provocative *limb* and, we are to believe, to drape piano legs with little skirts, fearing that the sight of a nicely-turned piece of mahogany might over-excite the vicar. Nineteenth-century writing was massively influenced by the prevailing prudery of the time. The Reverend Sabine Baring-Gould, most famous for penning 'Onward Christian Soldiers', was clearly the type likely to be disturbed by the sight of a bare piano leg. He conducted his own personal war against salaciousness, writing about 'certain heavily-frilled cotton investitures of the lower limbs' when he meant petticoats, or the 'bloomer arrangement in the nether latitude'. Was he joking?

Most parts of the male and female body were never directly referred to at all in these times, even in the most euphemistic style. For writers like Dickens, bosoms were objects upon which dying husbands could rest their heads. A rare example of a reference to breasts in a sexual context appears in Thackeray's *Vanity Fair*. Dr Quills is talking to Mr Clump about Becky Sharp: 'Green eyes, fair skin, pretty figure, *famous frontal development*.' Well really, Dr Quills!

Linguistic coyness was not invented by the Victorians. In 1818, Thomas Bowdler, doctor of medicine, philanthropist and man of letters, published his highly popular but misspelled *Family Shakspeare*, in which much of the more 'colourful' language from the bard's plays was expurgated or paraphrased to avoid disturbing the delicate sensibilities of the time. Bowdler aimed to provide an edition of Shakespeare's plays that would be suitable for a father to read aloud to his family without fear of corrupting their minds. He sought to preserve all of Shakespeare's 'beauties' without the 'blemishes'.

For example, in *Othello*, 'Thy bed, lust-stain'd, shall with lust's blood be spotted' became 'Thy bed, now stain'd, shall with thy blood be spotted'; and in *Hamlet*, 'He that hath kill'd my king and whor'd my mother' became 'He that hath kill'd my king and seduc'd my mother.' Elsewhere, passages were simply removed from the text. Thus, 'Royal wench! / She made great Caesar lay his sword to bed: / He ploughed her, and she cropp'd' (*Antony and Cleopatra*) appeared in Bowdler's text as: 'Royal wench! / She made great Caesar lay his sword to bed.'

Dr Bowdler undoubtedly helped to bring Shakespeare to a wider audience at the time, but it's hard to forgive him for removing the earthy richness of 'he ploughed her, and she cropp'd'. Wouldn't it make an excellent substitute for the 'congratulations on the birth of your new baby' inscriptions in modern greetings cards? Anyway, Bowdler wasn't the only person to re-write classic texts for family consumption. Other writers, before and after him, were assiduously applying a blue pencil to works by Chaucer, Dryden, Burns and Milton. Not even the Bible escaped. But then they were a coarse-mouthed bunch, those apostles.

Even in our relatively enlightened modern times, we still run scared from a wide range of words and expressions, particularly those relating to sex, illness, bodily functions, disease and – the taboo of all taboos – death. John Betjeman, in his poem 'Churchyards', worried that we were getting more, rather than less, squeamish about describing what has happened to those that Shakespeare would have referred to as having 'shuffled off this mortal coil'.

Oh why do people waste their breath
Inventing dainty names for death?
On the tombstone of the past
We do not read 'At peace at last'
But simply 'died' or plain 'departed.'

Maybe not 'departed'. It too strongly conjures up images of the railway station. 'The train now departing on platform four ...' But then again, perhaps the train is heading for 'a better place'. And British Rail did once tell us that 'InterCity makes the going easy'.

We start our hand-written letter of condolence to our bereaved friend or relative with the words: 'I was so sorry to hear that Peter had died.' This is quickly torn up to be replaced by a second version which reads: 'I was so sorry to hear the sad news about Peter.' It's as if we think by avoiding a particular word, we can spare the grieving wife a rude reminder that her husband is dead.

And we really don't like 'killing' anything – even animals. Mad dogs are put down (or occasionally destroyed); pets, of course, are 'put to sleep'. It would be a rare and rather insensitive veterinarian who informed a child that its sick and aged tabby should be 'killed'. And of course we don't like eating animals either. We would turn up our nose at a menu offering fine cuts of such fellow mammals as pig or cow or sheep or deer; preferring to disguise our carnivorous appetites behind words of French origin – pork, beef, mutton and venison. Though for some reason, and despite the efforts of Richard Adams's *Watership Down*, we're happy to eat rabbit. Fish and fowl, by and large, provide meals which do dare speak their name.

Our fear of death, and therefore our need to dress the grim reaper in a nice cardigan and slippers, is understandable, and our euphemisms, though coy, are rarely misleading. But things can get a little more baffling in the area of bodily functions.

What young boy has not been puzzled by the uncharacteristically grumpy behaviour of his mother, sister or aunt being put down to 'the curse' or, even more confusingly, to it being 'that time of the month'. What's going on? Those same small boys can be equally perplexed by being asked, when spotted fidgetting, if they want to 'pay a visit' or 'spend a penny'. And why do some men leave the room to 'take the dog for a walk' when clearly they don't have a dog? And who is Percy? And what is porcelain?

None of us, at any age, likes to go into too much detail about problems with our 'plumbing'. Even doctors will ask 'How are things down there?' or 'How are the waterworks?' They are, presumably, trying to spare us, or themselves, embarrassment. Doctors also insist, and this is perhaps by the by, on asking 'What do you think is the trouble?', which always makes me want to say 'Well, you're the doctor'; though I never do of course. I'm not wired to say what I mean.

And coyness knows no bounds when constipation strikes, as in the famous note from Willie's mother: 'Willie can't come to school because he hasn't been, I've given him something to make him go, and when he's been, he'll come.'

When did you last indulge in 'Ugandan discussions'? We've moved on to sex now, by the way. This highly oblique euphemism was coined some years ago by *Private Eye*, and emerged after a party (held at the time of Idi Amin's infamy) at which a female journalist was alleged to have explained an upstairs sexual encounter by saying: 'We were discussing Uganda.' Sexual euphemism has come a long way since the Bible's 'Adam … knew Eve'. However, it's still hard to beat 'to sleep with' for saying the opposite of what you mean and yet being quite clearly understood. And as for the number of euphemisms for masturbation? You could fill a book; as someone, undoubtedly, has.

Then there's the television wildlife programme narrator who tells us that a female eel is being 'attended to' by a succession of males. We know what he means, but it can still result in a moment's pause when a department store assistant asks if we require the same service. Sometimes sexual behaviour is disguised more artfully.

Janet Jackson caused uproar in 2004 when she performed live before millions of television viewers as a curtain-raiser to the USA's biggest sporting event – the Superbowl. Singing with fellow pop superstar Justin Timberlake, and in what most people recognised as a carefully choreographed moment, she 'accidentally' exposed her right breast. Afterwards, a spokesman for Ms Jackson described the incident as 'a wardrobe malfunction'. We're pushing our luck here, I think. A wardrobe malfunction is when the door falls off your cheap bedroom closet. This was a language malfunction concealing a publicity stunt. Now when Judy Finnegan, of *Richard and Judy* fame, exposed her still bra-enfolded 'famous frontal development' to a British television audience, it's much more likely that she was genuinely the victim of a wardrobe malfunction. Judy wouldn't lie to us.

Nowhere is the true meaning of sexual language more imaginatively concealed than in the lyrics of popular songs – a tradition which goes back to the 'squeezed lemons' and 'crawling black snakes' of songs by the Mississippi Delta bluesmen – and updated by rock groups like Led Zeppelin. In 'Shake, Rattle and Roll', Big Joe Turner wrote about his 'one-eyed cat, peeping in a sea food store', and both Bill Haley and the Comets and Elvis Presley got away with singing it. Chuck Berry's 'Ding-A-Ling' didn't fool Mary Whitehouse, but escaped being banned by the BBC, and 'Honky Tonk Angel' pulled the wool over the eyes of God-fearing Cliff Richard, who took it into the charts before learning, to his horror, that it was about a prostitute. A little bit naive of him perhaps.

* * *

One of the most taboo words in the English language has nothing to do with sex, or bodily functions, or even death. It's the word 'liar'. It has probably been the cause of more duels, both at dawn and in the law courts, than any other personal slur. We can tolerate, up to a point, being called incompetent, lazy, arrogant, or even useless in bed – but heaven help anyone who calls us a liar.

The 2005 British General Election was fought substantially on the issue of whether the Prime Minister had lied about his reasons for going to war against Iraq. Such an accusation could not have been made within the debating chambers of the Houses of Parliament, where members are strictly prohibited from 'charging another with uttering a deliberate falsehood'. Even in this stricture from May's *British Parliamentary Process*, the word 'liar' is carefully avoided. The punishment for making such an allegation is suspension from the House. Mind you, May also expressly forbids members from 'making disloyal or disrespectful references' to members of either House. This didn't deter Benjamin Disraeli from saying of his political rival: 'If Gladstone fell into the Thames, that would be a misfortune, and if anybody pulled him out that, I suppose, would be a calamity.' Or David Lloyd George on Sir John Simon: 'The Right Honourable and Learned Gentleman has twice crossed the floor of this House, each time leaving behind a trail of slime.' Or Denis Healey of Margaret Thatcher: 'The Prime Minister tells us that she has given the French president a piece of her mind – not a gift I would receive with alacrity.'

Messrs Disraeli, Lloyd George and Healey may have incurred a disapproving word or two from the Speaker for such comments, but would most likely have escaped suspension. It would have been quite a different matter if they had dared to suggest that a political opponent was a liar! Over the years, parliamentarians have developed a phraseology which gets around the problem by talking about 'differences in inter-pretation of the facts' and 'estrangement from the truth'. A speech by Aneurin Bevan once provoked Winston Churchill to observe: 'I should think it hardly possible to state the opposite of the truth with more precision.' Occasionally, however, when Honourable Members get particularly agitated, the four-letter word does slip out.

In March 2002, the then Labour MP George Galloway reacted to junior Foreign Office minister Ben Bradshaw calling him an 'apologist' for Saddam Hussein, by shouting: 'You are a liar.' After a tongue-lashing from Mr Speaker, both parties apologised to each other and suspension was avoided.

Galloway might have taken a leaf from the book of 18th-century playwright and member for Stafford, Richard Brinsley Sheridan, who, when asked to apologise for calling a fellow MP a liar, replied: 'Mr Speaker, I said the Honourable Member was a liar it is true and I am sorry for it. The Honourable Member may place the punctuation where he pleases.'

It's only polite

There are more ways than one to conceal true feelings. The British are renowned for hiding theirs behind a smokescreen of formal politeness.

There's the story told by the late, great Douglas Adams about how he went into a railway station cafeteria, bought a packet of biscuits and a newspaper and sat at a table. A stranger sat down, opened the packet of biscuits and started to eat them. Adams says: 'I did what any red-blooded Englishman would do. I ignored it.' Both men alternately removed biscuits from the packet until it was empty. It was only when the stranger left that Adams lifted his newspaper to discover his own, identical packet of biscuits. Only the innate politeness of both men, their reluctance to say what they were thinking, prevented a biscuit brawl.

A psychological study revealed that 85 per cent of British people, if bumped into in a crowd, will instinctively say 'sorry'. I'm not exactly sure how this research was conducted, but I have an image of a man with a clipboard stepping into the paths of pedestrians in a shopping centre, and making a note of how they respond. If 85 per cent say sorry, how do the rest react? How many clipboards did the researcher get through? Anyway, you certainly wouldn't catch anyone with even a drop of Latin blood deigning to apologise. But we are British and we don't like to make a fuss.

We will go to great lengths to avoid embarrassment and confrontation. Our reluctance to complain about food, for example, is well illustrated by the famous 'curate's egg' cartoon in *Punch* magazine back in the 19th century. It depicts a nervous young curate served a bad egg while a guest at his bishop's breakfast table. Asked whether the egg is to his liking, he stammers: 'Parts of it are excellent!'

Some modern dinner party guests would rather die than embarrass their hostess by admitting that they hate sun-dried tomatoes, or even that they are seriously allergic to an ingredient in the lovingly prepared main course. Newspaper columnist A.A. Gill, however, is made of sterner stuff.

Ten years ago, I wrote a piece about sending back food at dinner parties. If it isn't any good, I said, ask your hostess to take it away and bring something else. Perfectly reasonable. I told the story of the dinner party where I'd refused to eat a vomitous lentil bake and the other guests had risen up and said they didn't fancy it, either. In fact, the consensus was that the smart lady at the head of the table was to gastronomy what Herod had been to pre-school daycare. The article had the desired effect – I haven't been invited to a dinner party since.

That's what happens when you say what you mean. Much better, most of us believe, to tell a polite little untruth, a lie, and stay on the dinner party invitation list.

Lawyers and politicians are particularly adept at hiding their feelings behind a veil of stylised politeness. Calling their political or courtroom opponents 'the Right Honourable' or 'my learned friend' doesn't fool a lot of people, but their liberal use of the world 'respect' needs some unpacking. A sentence beginning 'with respect' normally indicates mild disdain for the argument about to be challenged; 'with great respect' implies derision; and 'with the greatest respect' suggests complete and utter contempt.

Outside of the courtroom or debating chamber, there is a range of situations in which we might choose to avoid saying directly and explicitly what we mean. We might dislike someone's hat, or hairdo, or … um … book, but don't want to offend with an honest response. A 'very nice' or 'interesting' will solve the problem – but it won't be the truth.

That a lie can be infinitely preferable to the truth in certain social situations was neatly illustrated in an edition of the innovative US TV sitcom *Curb Your Enthusiasm*, starring Larry David. He plays a character modelled very loosely on himself, and in this particular scene, believes he has been snubbed by some new friends.

LARRY (TO WIFE CHERYL): They know they invited us
to the concert. They are obviously deliberately not
calling us. How can I call them up and say 'we're
waiting for your call' and then they'll say 'well we
don't want to go with you'. They could at least lie
to us.

CHERYL: Right.

LARRY: I mean call us and lie. We don't want to sit here
like shmucks.

CHERYL: Yeah.

LARRY: A lie is a gesture. It's a courtesy. A little respect.
This is very disrespectful.

A lie is a gesture of respect. Make a note of that.

* * *

What does British politeness look like from an Italian perspective? Milan-based journalist and author Beppe Severgnini spent some months in London, writing articles for Italian newspapers and researching his book about the 'Inglesi'.

Beppe and I worked together briefly, and I remember him being particularly struck by what he saw as the over-politeness of the British. He felt that it probably hid real feelings, but he wasn't sure. He said he had been standing in a queue in a newsagents and started counting the number of times the words 'thank you' were spoken during the simple transaction of buying a newspaper.

It went something like this:

Englishman places his newspaper on the counter and
says: 'Thank you.'

'Thank you', says the newsagent. 'That will be 50p.'

'Thank you', says the Englishman, and proffers a £5
   note.
'Thank you', says the newsagent. 'Here's your change.'
'Thank you very much', says the Englishman as he
   leaves.

Five 'thank yous' to purchase a newspaper! How much real
gratitude was involved? Precisely none. Beppe pointed out that
a similar transaction in Italy would involve, at most, a couple
of grunts.

What really troubled Beppe was when he found himself
acquiring some of these verbal mannerisms and even beginning
to think and behave like an Englishman. It came to a head one
rainy afternoon when he drove back to his central London flat
to find that, for the umpteenth time, someone had parked in his
clearly-marked resident's parking place. Furious, Beppe took
out a piece of paper, leant on the car windscreen and began to
write: 'Dear Sir, may I point out that you are acting in contra-
vention of the ...' At this point he stopped and took stock of
what he was doing. Here was a red-blooded Italian who, faced
with these circumstances, should have pulled out his car keys
and scratched death threats into the paintwork of the offending
vehicle. Instead, here he was writing a note beginning 'Dear Sir,
may I point out ...' Within a month he had packed his bags and
returned to Milan.

Say as I say

The 1980s saw the emergence of a new and disturbing threat to
our freedom of speech, to our ability to say what we mean –
political correctness. Since then, however hard we try not to
offend, confront or embarrass anyone, we can still end up
being accused of breaking its written and unwritten laws. By

failing to keep up to date with received wisdom on how to refer to one or other minority group, we can get ourselves into all sorts of trouble.

Political correctness had its heyday in the 1980s and early 90s, when it had the power to generate some fairly absurd behaviour, particularly in the United States. In 1993, the Black Dyke Mills Band was booked to become the first British brass band to play at New York's prestigious Carnegie Hall. Then objections started to come in from groups representing black, gay and lesbian rights, demanding that posters and other publicity material be changed to read 'The British Mills Band'. Extraordinarily, the administrators at Carnegie Hall bowed to the pressure. Writer and broadcaster Michael Magenis observed at the time: 'What would have happened if they found out the band ate faggots and peas?'

In July 2005, a conference of the Professional Association of Teachers debated the proposition that the word 'fail' should be deleted from the educational vocabulary and replaced with 'deferred success'. It was argued that repeated failure, such as in exams, damages pupils' interest in learning. Education Secretary Ruth Kelly said that the idea deserved 'nought out of ten' and it was duly rejected by the conference delegates. Sanity had prevailed.

But just three months later came the news that political correctness, which had already seen off the Robertson's 'golly', was now threatening the traditional British piggy bank. It was reported that several high street banks were planning to stop giving the porcine money-boxes to children and using the image in their advertising, for fear of offending Muslims. There was no mention, however, of the risk of offending Jews or vegetarians.

And political correctness often damages the people it seeks to protect, as in the case of a 1992 memorandum from the US

Office for Civil Rights advising federal government employees about expressions which might cause offence, and suggesting alternatives, such as:

- 'Persons with a disability' or 'individuals with disabilities' instead of 'disabled person'.
- 'Persons who are deaf' or 'young people with hearing impairments' instead of 'deaf people'.
- 'People who are blind' or 'persons with a visual impairment' instead of 'blind people'.
- 'A student with dyslexia' instead of 'a dyslexic student'.

The memo particularly incensed America's National Federation for the Blind. At its next convention, it framed the following sturdy riposte, which is well worth quoting at length:

> There is increasing pressure in certain circles to use a variety of euphemisms in referring to blindness or blind persons – euphemisms such as hard of seeing, visually challenged, sightless, visually impaired, people with blindness, people who are blind, and the like … [They] are totally unacceptable and deserving only ridicule because of their strained and ludicrous attempt to avoid such straightforward, respectable words as blindness, blind, the blind, blind person, or blind persons.

> This euphemism concerning people or persons who are blind – when used in its recent trendy, politically correct form – does the exact opposite of what it purports to do since it is overly defensive, implies shame instead of true equality, and portrays the blind as touchy and belligerent.

> Just as an intelligent person is willing to be so designated and does not insist upon being called a person who is

intelligent and a group of bankers are happy to be called bankers and have no concern that they be referred to as persons who are in the banking business, so it is with the blind ... to the extent that euphemisms are used to convey any other concept or image, we deplore such use. We can make our own way in the world on equal terms with others, and we intend to do it.

No ambiguity or obfuscation there. A wonderful example of saying exactly what you mean. Interestingly, the RNIB in Britain conducted a survey around the same time to establish how people responded to the term 'the blind' compared to four alternatives: 'visually disabled', 'visually impaired', 'visually handicapped' and 'visually challenged'. Their conclusion: 'When we analysed our results we found no difference between the responses of subjects presented with the different versions ... in other words, it makes no difference one way or the other whether one is politically correct or not.'

Political correctness has been increasingly dismissed as a threat to freedom of speech, as 'social tyranny' or 'the creeping dictatorship of the Left'. Its influence is less pervasive in the new millennium, but it's still a force to be reckoned with, and still claims victims – like American chat show host Bill Maher.

Maher's programme, *Politically Incorrect*, was a late-night talk show in which a mixture of show-business and political guests debated issues of the day, and were encouraged to challenge received opinion and narrow-minded thinking in general. In the wake of the September 11 terrorist attack on the World Trade Center, Maher offered a typically controversial point of view. He said: 'We have been the cowards lobbing cruise missiles from 2,000 miles away. That's cowardly. Staying in the airplane when it hits the building, say what you want about it, it's not cowardly.'

Although some pundits defended Maher, pointing out the distinction between physical and moral cowardice, the show's major sponsors, appalled by the comments, withdrew their advertisements and the show was eventually dropped from the schedules.

That's what can happen when you say what you mean.

Out of the back of one's head

Not all untruths are lies. Much of what we say represents a clumsy and innocently inaccurate version of reality – for memory is a fragile thing. Each time we attempt to recall an event in our past, we are remembering not the event itself but the last time we thought about it. The accuracy dilutes with each attempted recollection, and our imaginations subconsciously compensate for the lost detail of our fading remembrance.

Witnesses to a bank robbery will regale the police with a variety of lurid but often conflicting descriptions of the villains involved and their modus operandi. And the difference between a description given at the scene of a crime and that given in court, months later, can be startling. But no one is lying. The witnesses are simply being human. A study in America of 40 cases where DNA evidence had cleared wrongfully convicted people showed that 90 per cent of the cases involved mistaken eyewitness identification. In one case, five separate witnesses had identified the defendant. Another study of 500 wrongful convictions concluded that mistaken eyewitness identification was involved in 60 per cent of the cases. In clinical tests involving simulated crimes, correct identification was achieved in only 34–48 per cent of cases. Witnesses are more likely to get it wrong than get it right.

A friend tells the story of how, while hiking in the Welsh mountains, she was passing a remote telephone box when the phone began to ring. She answered it, and was astonished to discover that the caller was an old friend dialling a wrong number. A great story, which she insists is absolutely true. However, her husband says he distinctly remembers the occasion when his wife was told this story by a mutual friend. Over the years, he believes, she subconsciously adopted this story as her own and now genuinely believes that the incident happened to her. So it is therefore, technically, not a lie.

I was having a few beers with a couple of friends the other day, and told the story of how, many years ago, I had been on a trip with one of them, and how we had missed our last train home. It was dark, so we pitched our tent on a nearby hillside. In the morning we discovered that we'd been sleeping on top of a rubbish dump.

> 'That never happened', said my friend.
> 'Yes it did.'
> 'No it didn't.'
> 'It did.'
> 'It didn't', he insisted. 'It couldn't have. We didn't have
> a tent.'

Oh my god. He was right. We didn't have a tent. I had imagined, or perhaps dreamt, the whole thing. But it seemed so real, and I had told the story so many times. It made me start to doubt all my memories.

By the morning I had reconciled myself to the fact that I had been the victim of some sort of false memory syndrome, and that at least I had not actually been lying. I switched on my computer to check my e-mails. One was from my friend. 'I've just remembered', he said. 'We did have a tent.'

Our often tenuous grasp of reality can lead us to deviate from the truth in other ways.

The dinner party conversation turns to talk of Europe and

the merits of the EU Constitution. You are out of your depth, but feel you have to contribute an opinion. You launch into an enthusiastic but wildly inaccurate assessment of the issues, concluding that, on the basis that they are allowed to take part in the Eurovision Song Contest, Israel should be allowed to join the EU. It's an impressive performance, but basically it's bullshit. Nevertheless, your dining companions seem convinced. Maybe you were right all along. More likely you have simply confused them. But you weren't lying.

The philosopher Harry G. Frankfurt, in his small but highly successful book *On Bullshit*, argues that bullshit involves carelessness or indifference to the truth, rather than a deliberate attempt to tell a falsehood, which categorises the lie. He argues that telling lies involves more 'craftsmanship' than talking bullshit, but that it doesn't necessarily follow that the task of the bullshitter is any easier. The liar has to know his facts; he has to know what is right, before he can construct a falsehood. The bullshitter works without facts, which involves less knowledge, but a greater level of creativity if he is to be convincing.

Is that what's happening in these following examples, borrowed from *Private Eye*'s Pseuds' Corner? The writers in each case are clearly not lying, but there certainly seems to be an intention to deceive the reader into believing that something profound or at least meaningful is being said. And my apologies in advance if, in fact, there is.

> This lecture will explore the 'chairness' of chairs. Chair typologies because of their generic familiarity allow formal investigation of abstract and social values directly through the visual and structural language of the objects themselves.
>
> 'Form Follows Idea', lecture to be given by Professor Maxine Naylor at the University of Lincoln

A black hole uses gravity to create a rip in space time, warping space time. When I designed my Black Hole Terrace, I used gravity to convey this idea. I designed it in such a way that you fall down into the terrace that you eat on. It's not just a representational image, but presentational. In other words it's interactive. You fall into the black hole, through the event horizon carrying your dinner into the white hole at the centre, and into another space time.

Charles Jencks, *Building Design*

This exhibition aims to question existing hegemonic structures of cultural, social, historical and political landscapes through the construction of platforms for discourse and spaces of tension via the recontextualisation of the geopolitical premise of the 'island'.

'Insomnia: Islandhopping 2002–2005' at
the Institute of Contemporary Art

Mind you, the fact that these examples appeared in Pseuds' Corner and, indeed, in this book, suggests that you can't bullshit all of the people all of the time.

CHAPTER FOUR

Lies for sale

> By the way, if anyone here is in advertising or market-
> ing, kill yourself. Kill yourselves, seriously. You're the
> ruiner of all things good. Seriously, no, this is not a joke
> … you are Satan's spawn, filling the world with bile and
> garbage … Kill yourself, kill yourself, kill yourself now.
> Now, back to the show …

The stand-up comedian Bill Hicks, not a man to pull his
punches, didn't like advertising and marketing people very
much. They have turned our planet, he told his audiences, into
the third mall from the sun.

It may seem like a rather jaundiced perspective, but when
you look at the evidence, it's hard not to agree with him – that
we have become the third mall from the sun, that is, not that all
advertising and marketing people should blow their heads off.

W.S. Gilbert said that advertising is 'merely corroborative
detail intended to give artistic verisimilitude to a bald and
unconvincing narrative'. H.G. Wells, more prosaically,
described advertising as 'legalised lying'.

We're assaulted every waking moment with brightly-
packaged spin, hyperbole and clever deception aimed at
relieving us of our hard-earned cash, often for not very much in

return. Salespeople bombard us with unbeatable, chance-in-a-lifetime offers; products which will reverse the ageing process, smooth out the ravages of time and make us irresistible to the opposite sex; products which will upload/download faster, enhance our viewing pleasure, amuse our friends; products which will go faster, last longer and eliminate waste; products which will make us sophisticated, virile, envied and fulfilled – and save us time and effort in the kitchen. No home, nor indeed life, would be complete without them.

Not even children are spared. In fact, they are prime targets. A four-year study by the American Psychological Association reported in 2004 that the average child watches more than 40,000 television commercials per year. Its unsurprising conclusion was that children under the age of eight are 'unable to critically comprehend televised advertising messages and are prone to accept advertiser messages as truthful, accurate and unbiased'. But are adults any more discerning? It appears not. We behave as if we must keep buying or, like the shark that stops swimming, we will surely die.

Deception in the marketplace can be blatant, involving outrageous lies, and it can also be subtle. We are often, for example, led to believe that we are getting more for our money than is actually the case. Not for us a small portion of chips; McDonald's, for a modest sum, will give us 'regular fries'. Who could resist?

Frank Packer wrote to tell me how, when travelling around America, he has often become disorientated by the language of fast food:

Midway through one of my many all-day drives I stopped in a McDonald's near Elmira, New York, to order a quick meal to go. After ordering the burger, etc., I ordered a drink. 'What size?' the seventeen-year-old behind the counter asked. 'Medium', I replied. 'We don't have Medium' was the response. It took a while for this concept to sink into my road-weary brain, during which the counter person offered no explanation and simply stood, waiting. 'No ... Medium?' 'We only have Small, Large, and Extra-Large.' 'Then ... I'll have the, well, middle one.' 'That would be a Large, then', she explained helpfully, as if to someone not quite familiar with the English language.

Starbucks, not to be outdone, eschew the small cup of coffee and provide us instead with a 'tall' cup, and if we're a little more thirsty we can have a 'grande' instead of a medium. How generous of them. Actually, the largest cup available is for some reason called a 'venti' which is, I think, Italian for twenty. I asked staff at four of my local branches of Starbucks why it was called 'venti', but no one had a clue. STOP PRESS: A policeman standing behind me in the coffee queue at yet another Starbucks has just informed me that it's called 'venti' because it holds 20 fluid ounces of liquid. And policemen, surely, don't lie.

Furniture stores entice us with huge 'unrepeatable' price reductions on their expensive merchandise. A salesman at a branch of one large company explained how they were able to offer a £2,400 leather sofa for just £1,100 – a saving of nearly 60 per cent. Apparently they were required only to sell the product at its 'full' price for 28 days in order to claim the huge price cut. I asked if people who buy the furniture during the 28 days tended to get a bit annoyed if they saw it being sold a week or two later at such a reduced price. 'Yes', he admitted. 'They come in ranting and raving, so we make some sort of good will gesture.' So did he lose sleep over the fact that his job involved talking people into buying furniture at an artificially inflated price? He just shrugged.

The straightforward, unadorned truth is something of an alien concept in the world of advertising and marketing. The product all too often fails to do exactly what it says on the tin. And to a large extent we acquiesce with the deception. A Gallup poll asked people if they thought it was morally wrong for advertisers to exaggerate, for example, the cleaning power of a washing powder. Only 46 per cent thought it wrong or seriously wrong.

Complete honesty in the retail world is so rare that its appearance comes as a shock. It can seem as if we have wandered into a parallel universe. Just the other day I entered such a twilight zone when an assistant in GAP in London's Oxford Street volunteered the information that a line of jumpers I was admiring were prone to 'stretching and bobbling'. Quite a few had been returned by dissatisfied customers apparently. I looked closely at his face. He wasn't joking. He meant it. The jumpers were cheap and nasty and he wasn't going to lie to me. I was so astonished by his honesty I nearly bought one.

We'll look a little later at the psychology of advertising and why it seems to have such power over our behaviour. But first we should think about the extent to which we are being deceived.

Water world

Let's dip our toe into the water – into the marketing of water. We might suppose that something so essential to life would be free of such shenanigans. After all, our bodies are made up of around 70 per cent water – about the same as a banana, incidentally – and it's vital that we keep it topped up. In the Third World, thousands die every year for want of the stuff, yet here in the West, good old H_2O, still and sparkling, is bottled, packaged and promoted just like any other product, using every deceptive trick in the book.

At the beginning of 2004, Coca Cola invested £7 million launching its Dasani bottled water brand in the UK. Since the company advertised it as being 'as pure as bottled water gets', customers could be forgiven for assuming that the water had trickled out of an Alpine mountain or sprung from a huge subterranean lake. In fact, as it transpired, it came out of the tap at a factory in Kent.

Coca Cola made much of the fact that Dasani water went through a complex production process involving repeated filtering and something called 'reverse osmosis', a technique perfected by NASA to purify liquids on spacecraft. What liquids could they be referring to, I wonder? Finally, minerals were added to 'enhance the pure taste'. Nowhere in its publicity, or on the bottle, was tap water mentioned.

Coca Cola were by no means the only people distributing filtered tap water in bottles, but it was the firm's promotion of its product as 'pure' which upset the UK water industry, who complained that this implied that tap water was impure. The drinks company argued that the source of the water was irrelevant because it didn't affect the end result. 'There are different levels of purity', it said, 'and Dasani is as pure as water can get.' This, of course, is utter nonsense. There may be different levels of *im*purity. But pure is pure.

Things got worse for Coca Cola a few weeks later when the water supply at the Dasani factory became contaminated with a 'potentially carcinogenic bromate'. The company immediately withdrew all 500,000 bottles in circulation and ceased production. Dasani had lasted just five weeks in Britain. The newspaper headline writers had a field day. 'Eau Dear!' was my particular favourite.

Now, Volvic mineral water does not come from a tap. It comes from France, from the mountains of the Auvergne. I've been drinking this stuff for a while now, but I don't seem to be getting the full effect promised on the label:

> Thousands of years ago the Auvergne volcanoes erupted in a spectacular demonstration of power. Nowadays the natural spark of volcanoes is harnessed in every bottle of Volvic. Volvic – filtered through volcanic rocks to fill you with volcanicity.

Maybe I'm not drinking enough of it. I can't find any information about dosage. Or perhaps it's just mineral water after all.

Non-pukka claims

When Sainsbury's renewed celebrity chef Jamie Oliver's million-pound contract to promote their supermarkets, I imagine they were hoping his wife Jules wouldn't repeat her indiscretion of being photographed shopping at their rivals Waitrose. They want to maintain the illusion – if not an actual lie – that Jamie's heart, and that of an increasing portion of his extended family, belongs to Sainsbury's.

The same goes for all the other celebrities paid to promote the value of products or services which simple common sense tells us they would probably never use in real life. Their sudden affection for a particular insurance company (Michael Winner) or credit card (Samuel L. Jackson et al) is far from convincing. Let me know next time you spot James Nesbitt leafing through the Yellow Pages, or bump into Linda Barker in Comet, or Neil Morrissey and Leslie Ash in Homebase. I need a lot of convincing that Naomi Campbell buys her clothes from Tesco. And how often would we find a packet of Walkers Crisps in Gary Lineker's lunch box?

Such seemingly transparent fictions are just another manifestation of the advertiser's art. My lawyers advise me that

I can't say that the following claims made for products are lies or are deliberately misleading – but they can't stop me thinking it.

First there's the classic: '**Eight out of ten cats prefer Whiskas.**' To what? Sump oil? We see the cat padding towards a selection of plates of (what appears to be) cat food. It goes straight for the Whiskas. What did they put on those other plates? We were never told. And anyway, perhaps the two cats who don't prefer Whiskas are intelligent, discerning animals with sophisticated palates; the kind of pets we would all like to own.

A television advertisement makes the following claim for a brand of moisturising cream: '**It is clinically proven: your wrinkles can look ten years younger.**' What does that mean? And what happens if your wrinkles are, in fact, already less than ten years old?

Spotted on the shelf of a supermarket: '**New Improved Swarfega Original.**' The manufacturer here is clearly attempting to both have his green gunge and eat it. And the manufacturers of TUC savoury biscuits are also at it, labelling their product '**TUC ORIGINAL – New Improved Recipe.**' But then they are crackers!

For £12.50 you can buy a set of '**Eternal Life**' rings on eBay. '**These rings are believed to allow humans to stay physically young forever**', we are told. But they don't actually say who believes this. Fascinatingly, the risk-free guarantee offered with these rings allows you to return them within 30 days if you're not entirely satisfied with your purchase. Tough if you start growing old after 31 days, I guess.

'**Ford cars – 700 per cent quieter.**' When advertising watchdogs asked Ford to substantiate this claim, to identify cars which were 700 per cent noisier than the Ford, the company explained that it meant the inside of the Ford was 700 per cent quieter than the outside. Just like most other cars.

'**British Airways is the world's favourite airline.**' Says who? The company was, in the 1990s, the most profitable airline in the world, but that didn't necessarily make it popular.

'No other hair loss product on the market today uses **the synergistic energy of maximum strength Habanero, bio-extracts, and Alpha Hydroxy, to retain hair and regrow lost hair.**' That's probably because none of those ingredients has any proven hair-restorative quality.

With advertising on radio and television, it's not just what you say but the way you say it. Top voice-over artists are paid substantial fees because their vocal chords are believed to have the power to sway people's judgement in favour of one tin of baked beans over another. It's a mysterious skill. An actor friend was once employed to enthuse about the merits of a particular brand of yoghurt. After about 40 takes he had still failed to capture the elusive, persuasive tone required by the manufacturers. 'How exactly do you want me to do it?' he finally asked in exasperation. 'Try to sound more yoghurty' was the hugely helpful response.

Another weasely advertising trick is to make claims, implying that a product is better or cheaper than others, using language which, under close examination, actually means next to nothing. It's a cunning way of circumventing the Trades Description Act.

'Our toothpaste *helps* fight tooth decay.'
Helps how much? Not much, probably.

'Our cough medicine *acts fast*.'
How fast?

'Save *up to* 50 per cent.'
This could mean a 1 per cent saving.

'Our product is now 20 per cent *cheaper*.'
Cheaper than what?

'*More people than ever* are using ...'
But the product might have previously been used by almost nobody.

'*Lowest price ever*.'
But is it a good price?

'*Helps control* dandruff *symptoms* with *regular use*.'
You'll still have dandruff, but it will be well-behaved.

Only well-honed scepticism and an eye for linguistic detail can protect you from such trickery. If the advertiser says 'Nothing acts faster than Anadin', your response should always be 'Then I'll take nothing'.

The watchdogs

With so many people out there trying to pull the finest home-spun Angoran wool over our eyes, we need all the protection we can get.

The Federal Trade Commission is responsible for cracking down on US companies that make fraudulent claims about products. It has had its successes, notably against a company which claimed that its 'Vitamin O' could prevent or treat cancer, heart disease and other life-threatening diseases. After the FTC told a court that the product was little more than salt water, the company agreed to pay $375,000 to its customers.

It was also prevented from making future claims that the liquid in Vitamin O could help the body absorb more oxygen. As an FTC lawyer pointed out, 'only fish can do that'.

In Britain, that tireless defender of consumer rights, the Consumers' Association, now formally known as Which?, keeps tabs on the companies who most frequently upset the Advertising Standards Authority by making false or unreasonable claims for their products.

In a 2005 survey, British Telecom came top of the Which? chart with 34 complaints upheld. It had, among other things, made unsubstantiated claims about the number of customers who had returned to the company and also wrongly implied that all its competitors charged for their helplines. Close behind came the Dixons Retail Group with 32 rulings. Dixons caused confusion over the resolution of a digital camera, mixed up inches and centimetres on a TV, and based discounts on higher old prices to make savings seem bigger. But Which? gave its prize for the most outlandish claim to a company called GUS Home Shopping. Its *Innovations* catalogue claimed to sell light bulbs that gave out 'healthier light'.

Which? is particularly concerned about the meaninglessness and duplicity of claims made about the health-bringing properties of products – that they are rich in vitamin C, build healthy bones, have 'no added sugar', are 'good for concentration' and 'help your heart'.

The March 2004 edition of its magazine reported, for example, that some vegetable cooking oils were being marketed as containing no cholesterol, making them appear healthy and less likely to cause weight gain or heart disease. In doing so, said Which?, the companies tricked consumers into thinking that other brands might contain cholesterol. But cholesterol is an animal product, so all vegetable oils are naturally cholesterol-free. The magazine also identified products marked as 'Free From Artificial Preservatives' which were still packed full of natural, but unhealthy, preservatives such as salt.

In June 2005, Which? reported that it had failed to get the European Parliament to agree to vital measures needed to clamp down on such claims. This means that products such as Quaker Sugar Puffs – which contain a 'staggering' 47 grams of sugar per 100 grams – could continue to be described as 'nutritious'.

And this is just the tip of a gluten-free, tooth-friendly, vitamin-packed iceberg. What we really need are products which are free from artificial claims.

The great organic food deception

The organic food industry has become very big business. Sales almost trebled from under £400 million in 1998 to £1.16 billion in 2004, and are projected to top £1.6 billion in 2007. It's become a marketing phenomenon. But claims made about its products deserve close scrutiny.

Up until the late 1990s, organic food was widely trumpeted as being tastier, more nutritious and 'safer' than the alternatives. To this day, people who buy organic food invariably give one or more of those reasons for spending, on average, 63 per cent extra for the privilege of a Soil Association-approved organic sticker on their pork chops or Jerusalem artichokes. But they are, many believe, succumbing to a grand deception.

I have no particular axe to grind about the organic food industry. I'm not in the pay of the non-organic 'conventional' farming community. I just think that the whole debate about organic food has become so riddled with half-truths, exaggeration and distortion that it's next to impossible to know what to believe – and, therefore, what to buy.

In 2000, the Advertising Standards Authority stepped in to prevent the organic farming industry and the Soil Association from making claims about the superior taste, nutritional value or safety of organic products. It said there simply wasn't the scientific evidence to support such assertions. And, according to both the ASA and the Food Standards Agency, there still isn't. In his retirement speech after five years as chairman of the FSA, Sir John Krebs questioned the motives of the non-profit-making Soil Association, pointing out that many of its members were organic farmers with a financial motive for promoting its virtues.

The Liberal Democrat peer Lord Taverne believes that people who buy organic products are 'the victims of propaganda and hype'. He says there's tremendous pressure on people to buy organic, and that 'to question the virtues of organic farming is tantamount to questioning the virtues of motherhood'.

The language surrounding the benefits of buying organic animal products is particularly deceptive. Clever and manipulative advertising over the years has given the impression that the animals involved have somehow lived a long and happy life, grazing contentedly in fields of buttercups. In fact, although organically raised animals have to have 'access' to the outdoors, there are hardly any regulations in place that deal with the amount of space the animals should be given or the amount of time they should be allowed outside. Animals living in many commercial organic farms are still crowded inside while having access to a small outside enclosure. Animal rights organisations say that in some free-range facilities the animals are packed so tightly together that most of them never reach the 'access to the outdoors'. In March 2005, the Advertising Standards Authority upheld two complaints against the Soil Association for distributing a leaflet describing organic farming as 'healthy' and 'more humane to animals'.

Meanwhile, research into organic food continues. One study on rats found that those fed on organic fruit and vegetables were slimmer, slept better and had stronger immune systems. Another showed that organic milk had higher levels of vitamin E, omega 3 essential fatty acids and antioxidants, which help beat infections. But many scientists, including those working for the Food Standards Agency, dispute the claims and argue that there is still no real evidence of any health benefits over ordinary food.

Great news for rats, though.

* * *

Money for nothing

It would seem I have a really good chance of acquiring a considerable amount of money – AS MUCH AS £250,000 – courtesy of those terribly generous people at Reader's Digest. Over a period of several months I've received a barrage of envelopes containing silver tracking code labels, golden keys, assorted sticky labels with YES and NO written on them and a letter saying that 'the fact that you are now in possession of this information is proof that your chance of becoming a prize winner is 100 per cent confirmed'. Blimey.

They also sent me an impressive 'Double Finalists Certificate' confirming that a 'valued customer gift award and the possibility of a £250,000 win are already reserved in the name of MR B H KING'.

Progress towards this pot of gold involved a fair amount of box-ticking, label-licking and, I confess, the purchase of a Reader's Digest road atlas. I was assured that failure to buy the atlas wouldn't damage my excellent chance of winning a small fortune – but I wasn't going to take any risks. Actually, I wanted the road atlas – and it really is quite good.

Just the other day I received another envelope from Reader's Digest, including what appeared to be a cheque. But in small print underneath the box containing the figure of £3,000.00 is the disappointing proviso: 'If declared the winner.' An accompanying letter from Mr Peter Brady, however, was heartening:

> As the Finance Director of Reader's Digest, I authorise the release of thousands of pounds-worth of prize cheques every month. Our records show that a major prize cheque in the name of Mr B H King has yet to be issued – even though we have had many winners from London South East. This may be about to change with the forthcoming issue of a personal statement in your name. I would like to ensure that we provide you, as a particularly valued customer, with every opportunity to win a prize.

And a little further down:

> You will ensure that you have the opportunity of winning this Special Prize and cashing the £3,000 bonus, by accepting our forthcoming book offer.

Another book offer! In the context, it's almost surprising that Reader's Digest are so interested in selling me books. I thought they just wanted to give me money. Why couldn't they just come straight out and say 'Look, we've printed a large number of these quite interesting books which we can offer at a very competitive price. Would you like to buy a copy?' Wouldn't that be simpler – and less disingenuous?

Reader's Digest is clearly working on the assumption that substantial numbers of people will choose to buy the books in the belief that doing so will, in fact, improve their chances of

winning the big cheque. Some people, confused by the misleading and often downright deceptive paraphernalia surrounding
promotions like these, actually believe their 'specimen' cheques
are real. In America, an 80-year-old Seattle woman postponed
surgery so she could be at home to receive her imaginary
$10 million cheque, and a sweepstake by American Family
Publishers led twelve people to fly halfway across America to
collect their non-existent multi-million-dollar prize.

And quite often, people are the victims of actual skull-
duggery. British trading standards officers say 60,000 people a
year complain about competition scams in which they have
received letters, emails or text messages telling them they have
won a prize. The lucky 'winners' are then suckered into
handing over money or making expensive premium line phone
calls for next to nothing, or indeed nothing, in return. At best,
a prize might be one coach ticket to Paris, or a very cheap
camera, but the recipient has to spend more in phone calls and
'processing fees' than the gift is worth. The average loss to
consumers is around £50, but some have lost many thousands
of pounds.

As a general rule it's best to beware strangers, Greek or
otherwise, bearing gifts.

Asterisk and the small print

It's the advertiser's job to present merchandise, services or
special offers in the best possible light. Nobody expects anyone
to go out of their way to draw attention to the negative or less
attractive aspects of a product. We understand that, and
attempt to treat advertisements with a healthy degree of
scepticism. But we often fail to treat them with a healthy degree
of attention, being particularly poor at observing the small
print. The devil, as they say, is in the detail.

Virgin Atlantic, for example, was ruled against by the Advertising Standards Authority for claiming to be 'bigger than BA in the bedroom department'. It turned out that its bigger beds were available only on selected flights – a fact hidden in the small print.

Car showrooms take out full-page newspaper advertisements, displaying a range of shiny new models. In big red letters they proclaim that attractive finance deals of £150 a month and no deposit are 'available'. After rushing round to the showroom you'll discover that, while finance deals of that nature are 'available', they are not, as it happens, available for the particular car you want to buy. For that particular car it's necessary to put down a deposit of £2,000. But the deal still looks good – only £150 a month! Yes, but there's a final payment of £8,000. It's all there in the small print. You just have to spot it before you sign anything.

The small courts in Britain hear many cases involving aggrieved consumers who discover that their right to redress over a faulty car, shoddy workmanship or a terrible holiday are denied them by small print clauses in contracts. Sometimes the consumer wins, if the clause is deemed unfair, but more often the trader triumphs. Had I read the small print in my travel insurance back in 1984, I could have saved myself the trouble of submitting a claim for a pair of very expensive spectacles I had carelessly dropped on the upper slopes of Mount Etna. My policy expressly, but minutely, excluded spectacles, a clause I had failed to spot even before I lost my glasses. So if you happen to be holidaying in Sicily ...

The revenge of the cold-called

A whole new bagful of devious and deceptive tricks are deployed by that new plague of the communication age – the cold callers. These are the people whose calls cut short your much needed lie-in, drag you from the shower or interrupt your family meal – and they are, of course, never trying to sell you anything.

I know, I know, they're just trying to do their job, they're just obeying orders; but it doesn't make their persistent intrusions any less irritating. I work at home a lot, so I know these people. They're not only a nuisance, they're liars, working from cunningly prepared scripts designed to con you into listening to their weasel words.

They might start by saying 'Hi, my name is John and I'm ringing from the Bowater Group.' They're actually ringing from one of its subsidiary companies, Staybrite Windows, but don't wish to reveal too soon that they're trying to sell you double-glazing. Or they open with 'Hi, this is just a courtesy call.' It is in fact the complete opposite. They're phoning for entirely commercial reasons, but failing to offer you the courtesy of being honest about it. You should immediately ask them to do you the courtesy of not disturbing you at home, or ask for their home number and offer to ring at your convenience (suggesting this might be at 4 a.m.).

Another handy tip for getting rid of double-glazing cold callers is to tell them you live in an igloo. I tried this on one occasion and was met with stunned silence. Then I could hear the caller turn to a colleague and say: 'He says he lives in an igloo.' He came back on line and asked, 'What do you mean you live in an igloo?' 'You know, an igloo – no windows.' 'No windows?' I put the phone down.

One of the cold callers' tricks is to assure you that they are not, in fact, cold calling; claiming that you've ticked a box on a form somewhere inviting them to contact you. This is almost certainly a lie. Or they suggest that you've filled in one of their questionnaires. No. On an aeroplane perhaps? No. Sometime in the last fourteen months? No. Well, perhaps it was your wife? Goodbye.

You may be told that a particular company are looking for showhouses in your area to display their handiwork at double-glazing, burglar alarm installation or roof repairs. You will naturally assume that you're going to be offered some extraordinarily advantageous deal. Don't be fooled; there's no discount available.

Perhaps you might like to apply my father's foolproof technique for seeing off Mormons and Jehovah's Witnesses. He would say 'I'm a believer in the infinite universe and my religion forbids me to speak to you.' It works with cold callers too.

Cold callers have to obey one inviolable rule. While striving to keep the potential customer on the phone for as long as possible, they must not, under any circumstances, put down the receiver themselves. I claim a major victory over the telephone pests, having succeeded in manoeuvring the following exchange. I haven't made this up (apart from the name of the insurance company, which I can't recall).

COLD CALLER: Hello, I'm calling from the Cheap and Nasty Motor Insurance Company …

ME: I'm sorry. I'm busy. I really don't have time for cold callers.

CC: But I'm not trying to sell you anything.

ME: You're not?

CC: No.

ME: So why are you ringing?

CC: To save you money on your car insurance.

ME: So you want to sell me car insurance.

CC: Well, we're confident we can offer you motor insurance at a lower rate than you are currently paying.

ME: So you do want to sell me car insurance.

CC: Well yes, but …

ME: But you said you weren't trying to sell me anything.

CC: Yes, but we're trying to save you money.

ME: But you ARE trying to sell me something.

CC: Yes but …

ME: So why did you tell me you weren't trying to sell me anything?

CC (exasperated): Look, I don't have time for this.
    [SLAMS DOWN PHONE]

Result.

If you live in the UK, you may appreciate the following little tip. Get in touch with the Telephone Preference Service (TPS) via their website, www.tpsonline.org.uk. Follow their simple instructions to register your phone number free of charge. Under the Privacy and Electronic Communications (EC Directive) Regulations 2003, it's unlawful to make unsolicited direct marketing calls to individuals who have indicated that they do not want to receive such calls. All cold calling should cease within 28 days. Now wasn't that alone worth the price of this book?

The promotional lie

Here are a few shocking truths. The bearded lady in the freak show … is a man. The wrinkled crone who peers into her crystal ball to predict your future is just a wrinkled crone. The tallest man in the world is probably two men.

Phineas T. Barnum made a fortune from foisting these kinds of deceptions on a gullible American public. In 1835 he generated nationwide publicity after announcing that the former black slave Joice Heth was 161 years old and had once been a nurse to George Washington. When the public began to lose interest, Barnum announced that Heth was not a human being at all, but a mechanical automaton. When she eventually died, Barnum, having reverted to his original story, staged a public autopsy to verify Heth's great age. It backfired when the doctor announced she could not have been a day over 80. Not that Barnum cared; he had made a fortune.

The publicist Mark Borkowski has built a successful company with clients ranging from Selfridges to Amnesty International and including Cirque du Soleil. But he learned early in his career what tangled webs can be woven, once deception is first practised. It happened when he was acting for the Theatre Royal in London's Stratford East. In the best tradition of his hero P.T. Barnum, he was trying to stoke up press interest in a stagnant weekly talent night.

'What I used to do was improvise', explains Borkowski. 'I would ring a journalist and say whatever came into my head. On this occasion I rang the local newspaper and told a reporter that I had a fantastic new act – a dog act. Oh yes, what does it do? Um, it … er … tap dances. Really? Yes. How does it do that? Little iron clogs – dances to the theme tune to *The Streets of San Francisco*. Fantastic, I'll send a photographer around now.'

Borkowski had to very quickly acquire a dog – not a big problem for a man of his resources. He managed to borrow a small dog called Josie, owned by Anna Karen, the actress who played Olive in *On The Buses*, and then knocked up a set of canine tap dancing shoes. The *Newham Recorder* photographer duly came round and took a picture. It made the front page. Success. Punters would cope with the disappointment of the non-appearing tap dancing dog.

But Mark hadn't foreseen that the story would get picked up by the national press and TV's *That's Life*. Everyone wanted to see the dog dance. 'I was in trouble then. To be caught out as a liar would be the death of my career. So I rang up the *Newham Recorder* reporter and said the tap dancing dog had been run over in Windmill Lane – by a refrigerator truck. It again made the front page: TAP DANCING DOG DIES.'

But how could Borkowski justify such a pack of lies?

'I wasn't lying', he insists. 'Publicists never lie. I was simply being creative with the truth. I don't think I have ever told a lie in my life.'

I think he almost believes it himself.

A little while afterwards, residents of Windmill Lane launched a campaign to stop it being used as a cut-through by heavy goods vehicles. They stood in the road, waving placards declaring 'Tap dancing dog today – children tomorrow'. Borkowski sees this as absolute justification of his being 'creative with the truth'. His fictitious tap dancing dog would save children's lives!

Publicist Max Clifford has never, to the best of my knowledge, claimed that his lies saved lives, though they have made a great deal of money for his clients and himself. Clifford's credits include the classic 'Freddie Starr Ate My Hamster', a fictitious story planted solely to revive the comedian's flagging career in the mid-1980s.

Described by former Tory minister David Mellor as 'the sleazebag's sleazebag', Clifford at least admits that his relationship with the truth is somewhat elastic. 'Lies and deceit', he says, 'play an important role in public relations.'

An honest liar.

Caught by the testimonials

Another form of creative fiction can be detected in the testimonials used in the promotion of books, films and stage shows.

In her book *A Little Light Friction*, Val Hennessy recalls how she was once quoted on the cover of a new paperback release, *Who's Really Who* by Richard Compton Miller. She was reported as saying 'People will rush out and buy this book.' What she had actually written was 'Only totally moronic people will rush out and buy this book.'

Then there's the one about the famous author who submitted a less than flattering review of a book due for publication on 2 January, including the dismissive comment that it was, at least, the 'best book I have read all year'. It was, of course, reproduced on the dust jacket of the book without reference to its original ironic context.

Even I, your scrupulously honest author, am guilty of taking part in a promotional fiction. Mind you, I was only five at the time. It was a newspaper advertisement for Shredded Wheat, a framed copy of which hangs on my study wall to this day. It's 1957 and there I am, running in a seaside holiday camp relay race, baton in hand, the opposition nowhere to be seen, the wind blowing through my hair. 'Meet Brian Harry King', it reads. 'This sturdy little Shredded Wheater already has a man-sized appetite for Shredded Wheat.' The sad truth is that, according to my mother, I was actually trailing in last place as the picture was taken. At least the advert didn't claim I was 160 years old.

* * *

Like lambs to the department store

Drew Eric Whitman wants to share what he has learned during his many years in the American advertising business. 'Do you want to know the secrets of creating killer ads, brochures and sales letters that today's highest-paid advertising professionals use to bring in millions of dollars for their clients?' he asks.

For just $119.95 plus shipping, he will send you a four audio CD pack and 96-page manual containing all the information you need to make people 'buy like crazy'. That's all very well, but aren't there already enough people out there trying to make us 'buy like crazy' without Drew Eric Whitman creating more?

Past generations of advertisers with their clever half-truths and lies have turned our species into buying machines. The individual advertiser's objective is mainly to make us select one product rather than another, of course – but it still fuels the consumer feeding frenzy.

The question is, why don't we just stick our heads out of the window and yell: 'We're mad as hell and we're not going to buy this any more'? The answer is because most of the time we're entirely oblivious to what's being done to us. We are mere rabbits caught in the headlights of the marketing juggernaut.

As far back as 1908, in his book *The Psychology of Advertising*, Walter Dill Scott was advocating the then controversial view that consumer response to advertising was *non*-rational. He said that, to be effective, advertising had to make a strong impression, appealing less to consumers' understanding than to their wishes and desires.

Now, Richard Taflinger, a psychologist at Washington State University, develops the argument. He says that the act of purchasing a product is affected by both the conscious and subconscious levels of the mind.

Deep down inside every one of us we carry the baggage of the past, the unconscious reactions to stimuli, the ones that kept our ancestors alive, let them reproduce, let them gather resources more efficiently than their competition. All of these biological necessities, self-preservation, sex, and greed, still influence our reactions to stimuli, no matter how much we think our reactions are arrived at consciously ... By presenting the stimuli through the use of words and images, advertising can trigger the reactions in much the same way that reality does ... If an ad can make it appear that buying the product can improve a person's chance of staying alive, reproducing, gathering resources, improving their self-esteem, having more fun, be more constructive, destructive, answer questions, be able to imitate desirable abilities or appearances, or help others, then the consumer may be more likely to buy the product.

Our primary instinct is for survival, but the urge to reproduce is not far behind. The marketing world has clearly noticed this, which explains why adverts for almost every imaginable product, from furniture polish to high-powered assault rifles, incorporate liberal amounts of sex.

The girl leans forward, exposing copious amounts of cleavage. The headline reads: 'This is Debbie. She wants you to have this pair in your car.' The advertisement is actually trying to interest you in the grease guns the model is holding in each hand.

The psychological wisdom behind this is that, by showing women in a false state of arousal, advertisers are able to associate their products with sexual pleasure. In 65 per cent of print ads, women are shown with open mouths, their pupils digitally enlarged to imply arousal. This, says Richard Taflinger, gives a man the 'good to go' signal, making him receptive to the immediacy of the image, and to the advertising campaign itself. Are we men really so easily manipulated? God help us.

Women have different biological instincts and look for sexual partners who can provide for their offspring. Ads depicting men as wealthy, powerful and intelligent will attract women to a product, particularly if a bit of romance is thrown in. Showing a man in the early stages of arousal is actually counter-productive, because women see that as aggressive and threatening. Men, however, just want sex.

Two men walk through the desert. One opens a suitcase and a full-sized swimming pool (complete with water) inflates. They sit by the pool and a beautiful woman in a bathing suit serves them beer. When the second man asks where she came from, the first holds up a second small suitcase.

This particular brand of beer, implies the ad, gives men power over women. It also suggests that women are mere blow-up toys designed to serve men. It's a cunning deception of course, a total lie – and disrespectful to women to boot. Drinking beer doesn't help you attract women. Quite the opposite, in reality.

This advertisement, and numerous others like it, creates the illusion that glamorous women are included as a sort of special free gift with every can, packet or tin. Other advertisements for different products promise gifts of happiness, popularity or eternal youth. The only constant is that whatever we buy, at whatever cost, the free gift never materialises.

Perhaps Bill Hicks was right.

Is there any hope?

A listener to BBC Radio 3 saw a poster promoting 'a live concert every night' on the network. She tuned in and was dismayed to discover that what was being broadcast was, in fact, a pre-recorded live concert. She complained to the Advertising Standards Authority. In its defence, the BBC argued that live music was generally understood to mean music recorded live rather than music commercially recorded in a studio.

To me this sounds like a lie to defend a lie. It was, at the very least, disingenuous of the BBC to pretend that there was no

distinction between broadcasting a live concert and broadcasting a recording of a live concert. The Adverting Standards
Agency ordered the BBC to change the poster.

The ASA is at the front line of our defence against the lies
and deceptions of advertising and marketing but, according to
Which?, it offers too little protection and is toothless and
ineffective in many situations.

Which? is far from happy with the results of many of the
cases of advertising excess and inaccuracy that it has brought
to the attention of the ASA. The cut-price airline EasyJet, for
example, ran advertisements boasting that its flights were tax-
free for a limited time, but omitted to mention that there were
still taxes levied by the destination countries. Says Which?:
'EasyJet first pulled this trick in 2003 and, after we complained, the ASA agreed it was misleading. It informally asked
EasyJet not to run the ad again. The following year, EasyJet ran
an almost identical advert.'

Which? points out that the ASA operates by consensus and
persuasion – if an advertiser persists in breaking the rules, there
isn't much it can do. It can ask publishers to refuse to carry an
ad; it can ask to scrutinise the revised ad; and it can ask trade
bodies to expel companies. What it can't do is ban ads or issue
fines.

Until tougher laws and more powerful regulators and
watchdogs are established, we remain at the mercy of the often
deceptive and misleading language of the advertising and
marketing industry.

But there is hope. There are some companies out there
prepared to be honest, or at least to exercise restraint in the
claims they make for their products. Among them are the manufacturers of the Craftmatic bed. A television promotion running
in America promises purchasers 'a lifetime of temporary relief'.

Ahhh! That's better.

CHAPTER FIVE

It's just business

In the business world, honesty is rarely the best policy.

Gerald Ratner learned this back in 1991 when, after a lunch at the Institute of Directors, he informed his astonished audience that a pair of his company's earrings, at 99p, cost less than an M&S sandwich – but the sandwich would last longer.

Ploughing on, he explained that the Ratners jewellery empire, founded by his father, was able to sell a decanter and six brandy glasses for £4.95 because it was 'total crap'. Ratner paid a heavy price for his candidness. Outraged customers boycotted his high street stores, wiping £500m from the value of the business. He resigned in disgrace.

When Ratner took over the family concern back in the early 1980s, he quickly developed a reputation as a hard-nosed businessman, famously saying: 'They didn't build the Roman empire by having meetings, they just went out and killed everyone who stood in their way.' He might have applauded the famous 'greed is good' speech by Gordon Gekko, the unscrupulous financier played by Michael Douglas in the film *Wall Street*:

> The point is, ladies and gentlemen, that greed – for lack of a better word – is good. Greed is right. Greed works.

> Greed clarifies, cuts through and captures the essence of
> the evolutionary spirit.

Gordon Gekko was a manifestation of the widely-held view
that businesspeople are ruthless opportunists who will do
whatever it takes – deceive, lie, cheat – to get what they want.
The successful businessman does not, ever, volunteer the truth
that his product is crap. Which reminds me that Scott Adams,
the American humorist and inventor of the cartoon character
Dilbert, put business managers at number one on his list of 'top
ten evils', just ahead of marketing men and two places above
Satan. He thought them responsible for introducing three
kinds of products into the market-place – Better Crap, Exactly
The Same Crap and Crappier Crap.

The axiom about this tough, profit-driven world is that
money and morals don't mix; that the concept of business
ethics is a contradiction in terms – an oxymoron. There's no
room in business, it's said, for scruples, conscience or the faint-
hearted.

Now I'm not saying that everyone in business is a ruthless,
manipulating, black-hearted liar. That Rupert Murdoch, for
one, seems like a very nice chap. But, by and large, successful
businesspeople do not 'get where they are today' by telling the
unadulterated truth. The advertising and marketing people
with their slick deceptions are but foot-soldiers in the corporate world of deceit. It's the generals, ensconced in their
boardrooms and Lear jets, making decisions which can have
dramatic repercussions for their staff, shareholders and personal
bank balances, who create the environment for dishonesty.

We'll look in a moment at the potential consequences of big
corporate lies, but first we must acknowledge our own role in
the business of deceit – and not just as victims. We are all
businessmen and women in our way, irrespective of how we

earn our living. We enter into business every time we buy or sell anything, pay for a meal in a restaurant, return defective goods, negotiate a salary or a raise, apply for a loan, employ a cleaning lady or claim on an insurance policy. Even in our dealings with our family, we fall into business-like negotiations: 'If you're quiet for half an hour you can have an ice-cream.' 'How about fifteen minutes, Dad?' Nearly all the principles (or lack of them) of the retail trade are in play at the car boot sale.

> BUYER: Are all 14,000 pieces of the jigsaw here?
> SELLER: Oh yes.
> BUYER: And that decanter and six brandy glasses?
> SELLER: Finest quality lead crystal.
> BUYER: And is there any guarantee with the remote-control car?
> SELLER: Just bring it back any time if it doesn't work. I'll be here.

Life is full of 'little bits of business', and it's in our role as pseudo-businessperson that we most frequently descend into deceitful and manipulative behaviour. Just as honesty cost Gerald Ratner his jewellery empire, it can work against our best interests too. As we shall see.

Deceptively dishonest

Of our many entry points into the duplicitous world of business, few are as stressful and traumatic as the property market. Buying and selling a home invariably involves lying, often on a 'deceptively' large scale. Everyone's at it – buyers, sellers, estate agents, mortgage lenders, surveyors, solicitors. No exceptions. All are guilty. Have you ever sold a house? How honest were your answers to questions about damp, traffic noise and neighbours?

Often the lies or deceptions take the form of a highly creative interpretation of the facts – as with estate agent-speak.

> Characterful and deceptively spacious, four-bedroom period property with original features. Close to transport links and local amenities.

Loosely translated, this is a small, three-bedroomed house (plus broom cupboard), with outside toilet, sandwiched between a motorway and a railway line and half a mile from the nearest shops. Oh yes, and it's falling down.

The 'deceptively spacious' bit has always puzzled me. Surely they're not saying that any appearance of spaciousness is a deception, are they? More likely it's intended to mean the property is Tardis-like, more spacious than it appears. But square feet or metres don't lie.

The worst of this kind of misleading nonsense was put paid to by the 1991 Property Misdescriptions Act. This prevents houses being described, for example, as having a private garden if, in fact, there's a public right of way across the land. But it hasn't eliminated all the traditional double-speak. Buyers should still watch out for these kinds of highly selective and misleading property descriptions:

- 'Easily maintained gardens' means a small concrete yard with a couple of flower pots.
- 'Mature garden' means jungle.
- 'Much potential' means it's a money pit.
- 'Secluded location' means it's in the middle of nowhere.
- 'Close to local schools' means you can listen to playground obscenities on and off all day.
- 'Near to motorway links' means it's underneath Spaghetti Junction.

- 'Borders on' means it's within a country mile of some dubious attraction or other. Also has shades of the tourism advert: 'Come to Germany – we have beautiful women, fine wines and great food; and it's all right on our doorstep … in France.'
- 'Convenient for local amenities' means there's a Tesco's hypermarket within a fifteen-minute car ride, traffic allowing. A bit like the travel agent's 'stone's throw from the sea', which requires the throwing arm of a javelin champion.
- 'In need of modernisation' means it's in need of demolition.
- 'Would suit DIY enthusiast' – Frank Spencer, but no one else.
- 'Charming' means tiny.
- 'Compact' means tiny.
- 'Bijou' means tiny.
- 'Cosy' means divide Bijou by two.
- 'Studio' means (and thanks to BBC News Online for this one) you can wash the dishes, watch the telly and answer the front door without getting up from the toilet.

But lest you despair, not all estate agents are dedicated to drawing a linguistic veil over the shortcomings of the properties they are trying to sell.

Filthy old house – fashionable Chelsea, preserved as of architectural interest, God knows why. Providing you have enough patience and cash, would make three bedrooms … The horrible patch of weed and refuse-infected earth behind would make a lovely garden, maybe.

Believe it or not, this is a real piece of estate agent advertising from the 1960s – an example of the disarmingly honest approach of the Roy Brooks agency. Roy is no longer with us, but the company which bears his name still occasionally employs this novel approach, as do a few other companies. Unfortunately the style has not caught on in a big way.

Deception in the property market-place takes many forms. In October 2003, the BBC's *Money Programme* revealed that many mortgage lenders were actually encouraging home-buyers to exaggerate their incomes in order to get bigger loans.

In February 2005, the estate agents Spicerhaart were fined £9,000 after pleading guilty to six offences under the Trade Descriptions Act. One of their branches in west London was carrying out a practice known as fly boarding – removing rival agents' 'Sold' boards and replacing them with their own. Six months earlier, Romans estate agents in Berkshire were fined £3,000 for putting up 'Sold' signs outside homes that were not even for sale. Two company directors and a further employee of Romans agreed to have the signs erected at their homes to help boost business. Rather worryingly, their defence lawyer claimed that putting 'Sold' boards outside unsold properties was a ploy used by dozens of estate agencies.

Buying a house is reckoned to be among the most stressful things that can happen in our lives, not far behind bereavement and divorce. If all parties involved were a little more honest with each other, it just might nudge the experience lower down the league table.

Only one owner

After house-buying, the second biggest purchase most of us make is a car. Here again we enter a world of duplicity. And again, before we look at the behaviour of the professionals, have you ever sold a car privately, or part-exchanged with a garage? Did you mention the little accident you had a year or two ago, or the knocking noise which only happens when you go over 50, or the door which occasionally jams? And in negotiating a price when selling or buying a car, were you completely honest about the amount you were prepared to accept or pay?

And what about that postcard you once put in the news-agent's window offering your clapped-out Cortina for £200 o.n.o.? What was that bit about 'nice little runner'? Such behaviour is little different to that of the professional adver-tising folk whose wrists we slapped in the last chapter.

Anyway, car salesmen (they are nearly always men) are a very particular breed – both the second-hand and spanking-new variety. These are the people who, while negotiating a transaction which will almost certainly net them a tidy profit, will tell you: 'I'm losing money on this deal.' And of course every second-hand car has only ever been driven in the past by a sweet old lady (it's always the same one), making her way to church and back. Australian car salesmen have even developed their own particularly colourful language, a jargon designed, at least in part it seems, to hide some of the secrets of their sales tactics from potential buyers.

A Japanese car, for example, is a 'rice burner', and a set of sheepskin seat covers is a 'Kiwi pack'. A 'poverty pack' is a car with no extras. A 'dunger' is a bad car. 'Fast glass' is electric windows. A 'hair cut' is when the mileometer has been wound back. Customers are called 'heads' – a 'rotten head' or 'rotten chop' is a customer with a poor credit rating. 'Burning a head' occurs when a salesman upsets a customer. A 'wooden duck' is a customer who doesn't haggle on price – like a sitting duck.

Similar language has developed among American car sales-men. People who can't make up their minds are called 'squirrels'. 'Flakes' are people who never buy. 'Strokes' are time wasters.

And, though it's completely harmless, my favourite is their name for a windscreen wiper – the rear wash/wipe variety. It's called a 'bidet'.

And things don't get any more straightforward once you've bought your vehicle.

Over the years, Which? has uncovered widespread deception (and incompetence) involving garage servicing, including the routine omission of basic safety checks, charging for work not done, and unnecessary repairs. It's estimated that, each year, motorists in the UK spend more than £1 billion on shoddy or superfluous work on their vehicles. In 2004, Which? booked 48 cars into garages for full services, and reported that a quarter of the garages replaced parts, like filters or spark plugs, which didn't need changing. Other garages failed to carry out essential checks on brakes and gearbox oil levels.

It has also emerged that garages are more likely to scam women than men. A piece of government research showed that garages were twice as likely to carry out work not agreed in advance on vehicles brought in by women – and that franchised (but not independent) garages would charge women up to 50 per cent more than men.

It's a man's world, alright – and, apparently, all the more dishonest for it.

Manager shall speak unto manager

Like car salesmen and estate agents, the general business world has developed its own language – management-speak. It's the language of 'down-sizing' and 'paradigm shifts' and 'empowering' and 'fast-tracking'.

This book, for example, might be described in management-speak as 'out of the box thinking at the cutting edge of contemporary wisdom, pushing the envelope of ideas and taking a helicopter view of the issues involved.' And, therefore, a bargain.

Australian writer Don Watson doesn't like management-speak, particularly when it spreads out from the corporate world and into everyday situations. In his book *Gobbledygook* he describes such language as an abuse of human rights which is robbing people of their sense, their culture and their tongue. He warns that it's leading to 'the grey death of the globalised world'.

That's a bit strong. Personally, I think it's all very fine, often quite clever and amusing in its place; but it can obscure meaning and mislead when used inappropriately or in the wrong environment. When a headmistress tells her staff (and this is apparently true) that it's time to 'prioritise our priorities – curriculum-wise', you have to wonder if she's really in the right job.

Management-speak can remove meaning entirely, as in the job description for a post in marketing, which asked for 'proven ability to deal with ambiguity in a rapidly changing environment'. I could do that. Management-speak, says Don Watson, can provide a perfect cover for doing precisely nothing:

> Keep talking about strategy and values and implementation and going forwards with your key performance indicators, keep workshopping and dialoguing and monitoring and impacting and having outcomes and you'll go home as a person on your salary in a dynamic change driven organisation should, exhausted.

When a company promises to deal with your complaint or request 'within a reasonable time frame', it is, of course, promising you nothing. Scott Adams suggests that the greatest lie told in the business world is 'I'll get back to you'. The managers in his Dilbert cartoon strip are the kind who deny lying to customers, preferring to call it 'nonfull disclosure', or who tell their staff that overtime is no longer 'mandatory', it's 'required'.

Everything about management language makes Don Watson spit blood. He points out that if a bank decides to bounce cheques that overdraw your account by more than five pence and charge you for doing so, it will send you a pro forma letter stating that it's 'changing the way we honour payments which will overdraw accounts, so we can better manage the way you do your banking with us.'

An antidote to management jargon was invented a few years back by Tom Davis, a scientist working for the American company Silicon Graphics. Called 'Buzzword Bingo', the idea is to distribute cards bearing a variety of management cliché words and phrases to colleagues attending long boring meetings. Here's the sort of thing:

empower	networking	think outside the box	go the extra mile	closure
cost-centred	multi-tasking	leverage	envision	goal-oriented
fast track	**BINGO**	singing from the same hymn sheet	out of the loop	client-focused
cutting-edge	ballpark	level playing field	paradigm shift	move the goal-posts

Each person crosses out the relevant word or saying when it's used in the meeting. The winner is the first to complete a line or an entire card and shout 'Bingo'. Buzzword cards, with all your favourite management-speak in a multitude of combinations, are now available on the internet. Go on, you know you want to.

The greasy pole

Many people have quite modest career ambitions, content to do an honest day's work for an honest day's pay. But others want more; they want to achieve things, make something of themselves, rise above the common herd, place their footprint in the sands of time – or at least earn more than Fred next door, with his Porsche and his holidays in the Seychelles and his bloody plasma screen television and …

To achieve this, it's necessary to start climbing the greasy pole. It is, of course, possible to make progress without recourse to exaggerating your abilities, taking credit for other people's efforts, lying and cheating. Possible, but difficult. Remember, once you have chosen this course, you put yourself in competition with a lot of other ambitious people. You may want to play fair, but do they? You find you have no choice; you must do whatever you have to do.

Step one is to get a decent job. A surprisingly large number of people adopt the Jeffrey Archer technique and lie about their qualifications. A few embellishments to the curriculum vitae can work wonders. Archer boasted in his CV that he had been educated at 'Wellington, Oxford, Sandhurst and Berkeley'. He failed to make it clear that he was referring to Wellington School in Somerset, not Wellington College public school in Berkshire, or that his spell at Oxford was part of a postgraduate diploma in education, for which he was unqualified, never having obtained his degree.

The popular fiction writer was challenged about this deception in an interview in 1999, just before he was selected as the Conservative candidate for Mayor of London.

DAVID FROST: Can you just clear up, you only, you never had three A levels and you had …

JEFFREY ARCHER: When I was teaching at Dover College, very kindly a master there said you should get a Diploma of Education, he said if you want to go on teaching, and so I went to Oxford and did a diploma which I'm very proud to have got; I have a Diploma of Education from Oxford.

DAVID FROST: The thing is, in terms of Oxford, the Oxford and Dover College have got CVs in which it's stated that you have A levels in English, History and Geography and indeed the letters BSc denoting a Bachelor of Science degree appear after your name in the Dover lists, now how did that happen?

JEFFREY ARCHER: I don't know and it's wrong, I only have a Diploma of Education from Oxford, nothing more.

DAVID FROST: But who put it in your CV?

JEFFREY ARCHER: I've no idea.

DAVID FROST: Someone else wrote the CV?

JEFFREY ARCHER: No, no ... I may have made a mistake, I often make mistakes in life, we all do. But I think if you're going to only have a saint for this job I'm certainly not your man.

This seems to suggest that, unless you're applying for sainthood, it's OK to lie to a prospective employer. So go ahead then. With luck your deception will never be spotted, and if it is, you can always bluster.

Other high-profile creative CV writers include Richard Li, the billionaire Hong Kong 'cyber tycoon' who upset his investors when they discovered that he had lied about receiving a prestigious degree from Stanford University. Apparently he dropped out before completing the course. It may not have affected his ability to make wise business decisions, but it certainly diminished his reputation for trustworthiness.

Just two weeks after her appointment in September 2000 as Manchester United's communications director, Alison Ryan was fired when her CV was exposed as fiction. To win the £125,000 a year job she had falsely claimed a first-class Cambridge degree and a distinction in her law qualification. She also forged a reference in the name of a non-existent lecturer from Manchester Metropolitan University.

In his application to become a Superior Court judge in Los Angeles, the distinguished Judge Patrick Couwenberg claimed he had been a covert CIA operative working underground in Laos during the Vietnam war and had been awarded a Purple Heart after being wounded in the groin by stray shrapnel during combat. In fact he had never worked for the CIA nor seen any combat. In August 2001 the 55-year-old judge was sacked after a commission on judicial performance found him guilty of 'wilful and prejudicial misconduct'. Couwenberg's lawyers argued that the judge was suffering from a condition called 'pseudologica fantastica' which caused him to lie uncontrollably.

These are not rare examples. A MORI poll a few years back revealed that an estimated 25 per cent of Britain's working population had misled their potential employer while applying for a job. Their lies ranged from false details of personal skills and qualities to exaggerated experience and salary. Three per cent lied about a criminal record. Forty-seven per cent lied about their leisure pursuits (in hell's name, why?) and 18 per cent of people interviewed thought it was 'necessary' to exaggerate on their CV.

Psychologists Liz Walley and Mike Smith, co-authors of *Deception in Selection*, argue that CV fraud is growing because 'people believe everyone else is doing it'. The development of new CV-checking technology may make it a lot more difficult to get away with this particular deception in the future. But we'll look at that in another chapter.

Once your embellished CV has been accepted, the next golden opportunity to exaggerate and invent comes in the job interview. In this environment, the plain truth is rarely good enough.

> INTERVIEWER: Have you much experience of rubber extrusions?
> INTERVIEWEE: Oh yes. Loads.
> INTERVIEWER: Can you give us an example?
> INTERVIEWEE: Oh yes. My home is a shrine to rubber extrusions. I subscribe to *Rubber Extrusions Weekly*. My every waking thought is of rubber extrusions.
> INTERVIEWER: And why do you think we should appoint you?
> INTERVIEWEE: Because I can take rubber extrusions to new and previously unimagined heights. I can broaden the horizons of the rubber extrusions business. I am Rubber Extrusion Man.

We've all done it.

Once any kind of power is achieved in any branch of the corporate world, it must be ruthlessly defended, by whatever means necessary, fair or foul. The greasy pole is, after all … greasy. As you work your way up the career ladder and gain managerial responsibilities, opportunities will present themselves to enhance your status – by taking credit for other people's ideas.

> CREATIVE: I've just had this brilliant idea for a television programme. You take a group of people and put

them in a house. You get half of them to paint a wall
and the other half to plant grass seed in the garden.
The public vote to evict people based on which
activity they find the most boring – watching grass
grow or watching paint dry. It'll be amazing.

MANAGER: What a coincidence. I had exactly the same
idea myself only yesterday. Well done, though. Great
minds think alike.

Bosses have been taking the credit for the work of their
subordinates for centuries. It's now known, for example, that
some paintings by the great masters were substantially the
work of their apprentices. Nigel Planer's play *On The Ceiling*
tells the story of the painting of the Sistine Chapel from the
perspective of Michelangelo's hired craftsmen, who complain
bitterly that all the glory is going to the 'whingeing Florentine
drama queen'.

Another way to keep ahead in the rat race is to scupper the
attempts of others to overtake us. Even the most unimaginative
middle-manager can normally place enough stumbling blocks
in the way of thrusting young newcomers to keep them in
check. If a potential rival is being considered for promotion, a
few choice lies whispered in the right ear should fix things.
And if the upstart is in line for a big job with a rival company,
you have a couple of options. If you want to get rid of him,
exaggerate his qualities in his reference. If you would rather he
remained under your thumb, mentioning clock-watching and
lack of initiative should do the trick.

Digressing only slightly; in many American states, job
applicants have the right to read reference letters and can even
sue for defamation if they don't like what they see. Economics
professor Robert Thornton came up with a solution for fellow
academics wishing to avoid litigation. He calls it his Lexicon

of Inconspicuously Ambiguous Recommendations, or LIAR
for short.

Some examples from LIAR:

To describe a person who is totally inept: 'I most
enthusiastically recommend this candidate with no
qualifications whatsoever.'

To describe an unpleasant ex-associate: 'I am pleased to
say that this candidate is a former colleague of mine.'

To describe a person so unproductive that the job slot
would be better off unfilled: 'I can assure you that no
person would be better for the job.'

To describe a total slackard: 'In my opinion, you will be
very fortunate to get this person to work for you.'

Corporate deception

'Falsehood ceases to be falsehood when it is understood on all
sides that the truth is not expected to be spoken.' This assertion
by 19th-century poet and statesman Sir Henry Taylor seems to
apply fairly neatly to a lot of business scenarios. Lying, as we
are beginning to establish, is essential to the task of obtaining
and maintaining corporate power and influence. It's also part
and parcel of normal business methodology.

In a famous article in the *Harvard Business Review* back in
1968, Albert Z. Carr (yes really) wrote:

Most executives from time to time are almost com-
pelled, in the interests of their companies or themselves,
to practice some form of deception when negotiating

with customers, dealers, unions, government officials, or even other departments of their companies. By conscious misstatements, concealment of pertinent facts, or exaggeration ... they seek to persuade others to agree with them.

Carr argued that the executive foolish enough to tell the truth would be ignoring opportunities 'permitted under the rules' and would be at a heavy disadvantage in his business dealings. He believed that this widespread dishonesty – or 'bluffing' as he preferred to call it – was played 'at all levels of corporate life, from the highest to the lowest.'

And if you're caught out in a deception, and confronted by an injured party, you can always resort to the ultimate defence. 'It's not personal. It's just business!' It's not personal? Of course it's personal. If it wasn't personal, why didn't they do it to someone else?

A certain amount of 'bluffing' certainly comes in handy when a firm is just starting up. Sometimes the deceptions are fairly innocent and harmless. Back in the late 1970s an old college friend took on huge loans to set up a public relations business. He rented a tiny office, bought a second-hand typewriter and a fax machine and then blew the bulk of the remaining cash on a Lotus Esprit. 'You have to present the right image', he explained. 'Nobody will want me to represent them if they think I'm struggling.' It made sense, although I happen to know he had wanted a Lotus Esprit long before he ever thought of going into business. Anyway, it seemed to work and eventually he made enough money to bring the rest of his lifestyle up to the standard falsely suggested by his car.

Nowadays it's as important as ever for the small business to 'project large'. One trick is to install a fancy telephone answering machine in the office, which will offer the caller a list of departments to which he or she can be put through. Whichever option is selected, the call will of course come through to you – the company chairman, managing director, head of sales, marketing boss, chief cook and bottle washer. Who could fail to be impressed?

When Jim Zona, the CEO of Pittsburgh Plastics in Pennsylvania, was starting up in business, he developed a ruse for selling his company's shoe-insoles to retail outlets. He would arrange for someone to visit a store and ask if it carried Gel-Soles. Two days later, he'd get someone else to do the same. After a few days, he'd have a salesperson phone the store to see if it wanted to carry his product. 'And they'd tell us to come on down', recalls Zona. A simple but effective deception.

But just as a little deception can help build you up, too much honesty can take you down. The American business magazine, *Inc*, publishes an annual list of the country's fastest-growing privately-owned companies. The CEO of one, un-named, company on the list was reported as saying that he had learned not to tell his employees too much. 'One time I decided to just be honest with our employees about our company's precarious financial condition', he recalls. 'I called all of my people together and said: "Look, we're handing out payroll cheques, but we're broke. If you have to cash your cheque, I'll understand. But this is where we are at financially. Could you guys just hold off cashing your cheque for a week?" All 40 employees ran to the bank that day.' Next time, he says, he almost certainly would not be so truthful.

The harder you fall

Lies and deception can get you started in business, can take you to the top and can sustain you in power. They can also bring about your downfall. Over recent years, some of the grandest fromages in the business world have come tumbling down to earth, their corporate misbehaviour exposed in the courts.

In April 2005, Rodney Adler, one of the highest-profile businessmen in Australia, was jailed for four-and-a-half years for his fraudulent role in the collapse of the giant HIH insurance company, of which he had been a director.

Adler had pleaded guilty to a variety of charges, including making false statements intended to induce others to buy shares in HIH and lying to obtain several million dollars from HIH for a company in which he had an interest. The trial judge said that Adler's offences displayed 'an appalling lack of commercial morality'.

Adler had argued that some of the charges to which he had pleaded guilty were the corporate equivalent of parking tickets. 'Why should I go to jail? For what?', he asked. But Judge Dunford said that Adler's crimes 'were not stupid errors of judgement but deliberate lies'. After his sentencing, Adler was more contrite, and admitted: 'I was a company director of HIH and I lied, and when you lie you deserve to be punished.'

Meanwhile, in America the business world had scarcely recovered from revelations of the lies and cheating which had brought the country's seventh largest company, Enron, crashing to its knees, when news of the Worldcom scandal emerged. Shareholders lost $180 billion when the telecommunications giant collapsed, and 20,000 workers lost their jobs. The company's boss, Bernie Ebbers, was found guilty of fraud and conspiracy involving $11 billion worth of creative accountancy. Ebbers told the court he knew too little about the company's accounts to be aware of what was going on, and blamed his former finance chief, Scott Sullivan. Sullivan, in response, said his actions were on the instructions of Ebbers. In July 2005, 63-year-old Ebbers was sent to jail for 25 years.

Britain, of course, has its own dishonourable record of

boardroom fraud. Robert Maxwell was born into abject poverty in Czechoslovakia, fled the Nazis in 1940, came to Britain and built a hugely successful publishing empire. He presented himself as a man of integrity, a man you could trust. In 1991 he provided a few words of calm reassurance to his worried Mirror Group Newspaper employees: 'Our company pension schemes are financially sound and well run.'

He was, of course, lying through his teeth. Following his mysterious death just a few months later, it emerged that he had been siphoning huge amounts of money out of the pension funds and pouring it into his companies to boost their share price.

Several years earlier, Ernest Saunders, the former chairman of drinks company Guinness, was sentenced to five years in jail for his part in a shares fraud perpetrated during the company's £2.6 billion takeover bid for rivals Distillers. His jail term was halved on appeal. He and other directors charged were said to have shown a 'contempt for truth and common honesty'.

Saunders was released from prison after serving just ten months, when doctors diagnosed that he was suffering from 'irreversible' Alzheimer's disease. Once free, he made a rapid and miraculous recovery and returned to work as a business consultant. What exactly were his new clients hoping to learn from him?

Cases of fraud and corruption in the business world seem to be on the increase, or at least are being detected more frequently. High Court cases are stacking up and there are even political moves to end jury trials in complicated cases, partly to speed up the process. So what's going on?

The very nature of business requires a tough, even ruthless approach. Gerald Ratner's Roman Empire analogy – kill everyone in your way – gives us some idea of the attitude or 'mindset'. While most businessmen will, when their backs are against the wall, baulk at inflicting wholesale slaughter, a few lies and a bit of deception might seem a small price to pay to protect the interests of a company and all its stakeholders. It's just like a parking offence, after all.

But criminal charges and imprisonment do not, as Ernest Saunders demonstrated, have to end a business career. American millionaire lifestyle guru Martha Stewart was released from prison after five months of her sentence for shares fraud. She had been branded a liar during her trial. The American TV networks were so shocked by her behaviour that they immediately offered her two new shows. Shares in her company began to rise rapidly. Martha's star was, once more, in the ascendant.

Perhaps business and ethics don't mix because they don't have to.

Fancies

You don't have to be a company chairman or director to develop a casual attitude to the precise ownership of the squillions of pounds slopping around in the accounts. Personal assistant Joyti De-Laurey thought she deserved her share of the fortunes being earned by her bosses at City bankers Goldman Sachs. Over a period of fourteen months she forged signatures to siphon off a total of £4.3 million, which she spent on a luxury villa in Greece, top-of-the-range cars, a powerboat, diamonds, flying lessons and clothes. De-Laurey, who had told her employers she was suffering from cancer in order to gain sympathy, told Southwark Crown Court that she felt she was entitled to the money for her 'indispensable services', which included covering up for one banker's extra-marital affair.

The judge who sentenced De-Laurey to seven years in prison in June 2004 described her as 'duplicitous, deceitful and thoroughly dishonest'. Her mother-in-law said: 'It didn't dawn on you at first that she used to lie. Till you'd known her quite a while, and then you could pick them out like sweets. The fibs she'd tell. Fancies! In the end I got to think of them as fancies. I don't think she ever knew she was lying.'

Of course, most of us know the difference between truth and lies and would never develop a 'contempt for truth and common honesty'. We have never exaggerated our qualifications, fiddled our expenses, taken credit for someone else's achievement. We are above reproach. Oh yeah? What was that one in the middle – fiddling expenses?

The facts are damning. According to a survey conducted in December 2003, one in five British workers admits to fiddling their expenses, costing firms millions of pounds every month. And if one in five workers admits it, how many are actually doing it? Because it's OK isn't it? Like lying on your CV, everyone else is doing it, aren't they?

A survey of 500 workers by the Pertemps recruitment company revealed that the most common form of 'creative accounting' was exaggerating mileage. Nearly 75 per cent admitted to topping up the miles on their expenses sheet. Claiming personal meals and drinks as client hospitality came in second at 40 per cent. One in ten admitted to submitting false receipts and 8 per cent marked up taxi fares.

Pertemps director Janet McGlaughlin said: 'Fiddling expenses is a natural temptation for staff and our findings show that it's a common occurrence in companies across the country.'

Fiddling expenses is a *natural temptation*! Well, if so, it's not the only fraudulent activity to which many of us are naturally tempted. But that's another chapter.

CHAPTER SIX

Read my lips

SIR DAVID FROST: Prime Minister, you are trailing in all the polls. A survey has revealed you are the most unpopular head of Government in modern history – and that was among members of your own cabinet. Your wife has announced she's voting for the Green Party and the leader of the opposition is, as we speak, measuring the windows at Number 10 for new curtains. Are you going to lose the general election?

PRIME MINISTER: Not a bit of it, Sir David. With the greatest respect, I was expecting to be behind in the polls at this stage. My unpopularity is what makes me a strong and effective leader. My wife is voting tactically to ensure we win a landslide victory and the leader of the opposition is washing our windows, not measuring them. I'm feeling very confident at the moment, thank you very much.

This exchange sums up the popular image of the politician – an answer for everything and the ability to argue that black is white. The truth tends to become a moveable feast, sometimes one abstained from altogether.

Political lies come wearing many different-coloured rosettes. Politicians are masters of the fine arts of obfuscation, dissembling and re-writing history. And they compete with journalists in their ability to take information out of context, subtly, and sometimes not-so-subtly, changing its meaning. Rising unemployment, inflation, escalating crime – all can be seen in a positive light, given enough spin. And political lies are never more apparent than at election time.

If he's prepared to lie to take us to war, he's prepared to lie to win an election

Michael Howard and his Conservative Party colleagues would not have been allowed to say it in the House of Commons, but out on the 2005 General Election trail, there was no stopping them. Tony Blair, they chorused, was a dirty rotten liar.

They were joined in their condemnation by Brian Sedgemore, a Labour MP of 27 years' service, who, just a little over a week before polling day, defected to the Liberal Democrats, accusing the Prime Minister of telling 'stomach-turning lies' over Iraq. His new party, ironically, resisted the temptation to use the L-word. Charles Kennedy may have thought it, but he wasn't prepared to say it.

Tony Blair spent the better part of the General Election campaign responding to allegations that he had lied to parliament and the country about the legality of the war. He told reporter after reporter that it was legitimate to question his political judgement in going to war ('It was a tough decision, but I made it'), but not fair to question his integrity. He had told no lies, he insisted.

History will probably give him the benefit of the doubt on this one, but you can't really blame the Conservatives for trying. Where they perhaps went wrong was in supposing that anyone would be remotely surprised that a politician might be less than scrupulously honest. This old joke says it all, really:

> A coach load of politicians were travelling along a country lane when their vehicle swerved off the road and crashed into a farmer's barn. The old farmer got off his tractor and went to investigate. Having surveyed the scene of carnage, he dug a deep pit and buried the politicians. A few days later a policeman spotted the crashed coach and asked the farmer what had happened to all the politicians. 'I buried them', he explained. 'They were ALL dead?', asked the astonished policeman. 'Well, some of them said they weren't', said the farmer. 'But you know how politicians lie.'

In the end, Michael Howard's repeated assertion that Tony Blair was a liar probably backfired on him. As everyone assumes that politicians are lying most of the time (How do we know when a politician is lying? His lips are moving), when one accuses another of lying, it smacks too much of the pot calling the kettle black. The restraint exercised by the Lib Dems probably served them well.

So should we assume that everything a politician says is a lie, in the expectation that we're bound to be right quite a lot of the time? Should we adopt the Jeremy Paxman approach and ask ourselves 'why is this lying bastard lying to me?' Or is that all a little too cynical? After all, politicians, like all liars, are only doing what comes naturally.

What, ultimately, is the difference between the behaviour of a three-year-old child who refuses to admit eating a chocolate biscuit and a politician denying he has taken cash for questions, or slept with a prostitute, or fast-tracked a passport? Our natural instinct is to protect ourselves from the consequences of our actions. Denial is genetically pre-programmed. When a politician denies something, we should look for the tell-tale smears of chocolate around his mouth and on his fingers.

Political lies are not just about denial, of course. They are also about false promises, spurious accusations, dodgy statistics and weapons of mass destruction. Political lying isn't a new phenomenon. In the early 18th century Jonathan Swift observed:

> Though the devil be the father of lies, he seems, like other great inventors, to have lost much of his reputation by the continual improvements that have been made upon him. Who first reduced lying into an art, and adapted it to politics, is not clear from history, although I have made some diligent inquiries.

Tony Blair began the 2005 UK election campaign with a major problem. His Chancellor of the Exchequer apparently considered him a liar:

> There is nothing that you could ever say to me now that I could ever believe.

It's the kind of thing you might expect a wife to say to her adulterous husband. The reality wasn't much different. They were the words of Gordon Brown, spoken to his political marriage partner, Tony Blair, as revealed in *Brown's Britain* by the *Sunday Telegraph*'s city editor, Robert Preston. Brown's angry declaration, we are told, was a response to Tony Blair's infidelity; the breaking of his Islington restaurant vow of 1994 to stand down and let his Chancellor succeed him as Prime Minister.

WARNING: The Tories will cut £35 billion from public services

But Blair and Brown were on their best behaviour during the election campaign, presenting a united front to the cameras, as at the unveiling of the Labour Party billboard accusing the Tories of planning major spending cuts. 'The cutting of spending by 35 billion pounds is equivalent to sacking every teacher, nurse and doctor in the country', intoned the Prime Minister.

At this, one of the gaggle of journalists observed: 'But the Conservatives aren't talking about cuts, they're talking about increasing spending, but at a slower rate than Labour.'

'Pleased you raised that', responded Mr Blair. 'We'll give you the quotes.' At which he turned to Gordon Brown, who pulled a crumpled piece of paper from his pocket and handed it to his Prime Minister.

Unfolding the piece of paper, Mr Blair told the reporters: 'Mr Letwin has announced that the Tories will spend £35 billion less over the lifetime of the next Parliament.'

'But that's not a cut, Prime Minister', persisted the reporter, speaking more slowly now. 'It's an increase in spending, but at a slower rate.'

After a distinct pause, the Prime Minister suggested: 'It's a cut over Labour's plan'.

The Tories retaliated immediately. Party chairman Liam Fox said that Labour's claims were 'at best misrepresentation, at worst a downright lie', and that the 'smear' tactics were a sign of desperation. This set the tone for the rest of the election campaign.

The business of spotting politicians' lies was made simpler during the election run-up by the introduction of a unique website, FactCheck, operated by ITN for Channel 4 and dedicated to establishing the veracity or otherwise of claims made by each of the main political parties. Its team of researchers uncovered some gems.

At one stage, a Conservative election pamphlet claimed that there had been 247 cases of the MRSA hospital virus in a single health trust. In fact, there had been only six. Informed of this, Michael Howard blamed it on a typing error. The numbers 6 and 247 are, after all, very similar.

On at least two occasions, Labour's Patricia Hewitt accused the Tories of reneging on a pledge to give parents £150 a week for childcare. In fact, the Conservatives had never made such an undertaking. When this was pointed out, a spokesman said on Ms Hewitt's behalf: 'That claim is not something that we are going to continue to make.'

FactCheck spotted lies and half-truths relating to the economy, health, defence, crime and asylum-seekers. The website was modelled on a similar one operated in America during the 2004 election tussle between George W. Bush and John Kerry. It too unveiled some pernicious political porkies.

During the campaign, John Kerry claimed that Bush was responsible for 'the greatest job loss since the Great Depression'. One Democratic congressman ran a TV ad condemning Bush for losing 'more jobs than the last eleven Presidents'. In reality, job figures were rising, unemployment was about average, and Bush had actually ended his first term as President with a small gain in employment.

Meanwhile, Bush was repeatedly claiming that Kerry 'voted over 350 times for higher taxes on the American people' during his twenty-year Senate career. When the Republican camp were pushed to list those 350 votes, the vast majority turned out to be votes *against* proposed tax cuts, not votes to raise taxes.

Sir Henry Taylor's observation that 'falsehood ceases to be falsehood when it is understood on all sides that the truth is not expected to be spoken', which we have already explored in relation to the business world, appears to apply just as neatly in the world of politics.

If in doubt – evade the question

When they're not lying (or, I suppose, telling the truth) politicians tend to resort to plain evasiveness.

In May 1997, Michael Howard, while campaigning to become Tory Party leader, took part in the following exchange with interviewer Jeremy Paxman:

> PAXMAN: Mr Howard, have you ever lied in any public statement?
> HOWARD: Certainly not.

It was part of the same famous *Newsnight* interview in which Howard persistently refused to answer a question from Paxman about whether he had, when Home Secretary, threatened to overrule the Director of the Prison Service, Derek Lewis, in relation to the suspension of a prison governor.

> HOWARD: Mr Marriot [the prison governor] was not suspended. I was entitled to express my views, I was entitled to be consulted …
> PAXMAN (interrupting): Did you threaten to overrule him?
> HOWARD: I … I … was not entitled to instruct Derek Lewis, and I did not instruct him.
> PAXMAN (interrupting): Did you threaten to overrule him?
> HOWARD: The truth of the matter is that Mr Marriot was not suspended. I …

PAXMAN (interrupting): Did you threaten to overrule him?

HOWARD: ... did not ... overrule Derek Lewis.

PAXMAN (interrupting): Did you threaten to overrule him?

HOWARD: I took advice on what I could or could not do ...

PAXMAN (interrupting): Did you threaten to overrule him, Mr Howard?

HOWARD: ... and acted scrupulously in accordance with that advice, I did not overrule Derek Lewis ...

PAXMAN (interrupting): Did you threaten to overrule him?

HOWARD: ... Mr Marriot was not suspended.

PAXMAN (interrupting): Did you threaten to overrule him?

HOWARD (pauses): I have accounted for my decision to dismiss Derek Lewis ...

PAXMAN (interrupting): Did you threaten to overrule him?

HOWARD: ... in great detail, before the House of Commons ...

PAXMAN (interrupting): I note that you're not answering the question of whether you threatened to overrule him.

Paxman repeats his question no fewer than fourteen times before giving up with a tired 'We'll leave that aspect there.' So did Michael Howard threaten to overrule his Director of Prisons? We will probably never know.

Psychologist Darius Galasinski, who has made a detailed academic study of politicians' language, has looked closely at the Paxman/Howard interview. He believes that Howard's refusal to answer a direct question, while falling well short of lying, fell equally short of telling the truth. 'Howard is trying to pass off his responses as good answers to Paxman's questions, trying to pretend to be co-operative', he observes. 'It is a form of deception; or at least of pretence.'

Interestingly, in 2002 Michael Howard told the BBC: 'I will never stand again for the leadership of the Conservative Party.' Asked if that meant he was ruling himself out completely, whatever the circumstances, he said: 'That's right.'

It must have been another Michael Howard, then, who failed to lead the Tories to victory in the 2005 General Election.

Saying what you have to say

The political career path involves climbing a pole as greasy as that in any other profession – maybe even greasier. Forthright honesty isn't the quality most likely to propel a budding politician into Number 10. Something a little less scrupulous is required. After all, the word 'politics' comes from the root 'politic', meaning artful, crafty or cunning.

The business of being politic begins when the aspiring politician seeks adoption as a prospective parliamentary candidate. Just how honestly do applicants answer questions about their reasons for seeking election? I've never actually attended a constituency party's candidate selection meeting, but I'm fairly certain it goes something like this.

CHAIRMAN: Why exactly do you want to be MP for Drudgetown West?

CANDIDATE: I feel a real affinity with the people of Drudgetown, and a passionate need to provide them with a voice in the Palace of Westminster. Their needs are my needs. Their dreams are my dreams. Their domestic sanitation problems are my domestic sanitation problems. Oh please, please give me a chance to serve them, humbly and dutifully, as the Member of Parliament for Drudgetown West.

Once selected, you've got to get elected, and this involves making promises. Does the general public really want to hear the truth – that times are tough and tough measures are needed? No, the public wants to be lied to. It doesn't want to know about fiscal imperatives and belt-tightening. It wants to be led by the hand, by a Moses in a grey suit, into the land of milk and honey and low taxes. The politician who tells it like it is isn't a politician for long – and promises can always be broken later. Digby Anderson, former director of the Social Affairs Unit, says that politicians don't tell the truth because the public prefers comforting lies. He thinks the public gets the politicians it deserves.

Once elected, only a great deal of verbal sucking up – saying 'Yes, Minister' when you mean 'You must be joking, Minister' – will get the average backbencher within a sniff of any real power or influence. The party line must be defended irrespective of personal belief. Every political opportunity must be grabbed with both hands. 'Northern Ireland, Prime Minster? Oh thank you. Just what I really wanted.' And once you've ingratiated your way into the Cabinet, how many lies might you have to tell to keep yourself from the reshuffler's axe – or from enforced resignation? 'But, Prime Minister, I've never even met the woman before ... well maybe I bumped into her once or twice at an official function ... well perhaps we did become quite friendly.' Finally, the admission that you are the father of several of her children is dragged out by the press and your unceremonious (though probably temporary) departure from political life rapidly follows. This is an entirely hypothetical illustration, of course.

That scourge of politicians, broadcaster John Humphrys, got himself into some pretty deep water in September 2005 when details of a private after-dinner speech were leaked to *The Times*. Among other indiscreet remarks, which earned him a 'rebuke' from the BBC, he apparently said of MPs: 'Those who do not lie at all ever ... do not get into government' because the whips 'won't go near you with a barge pole.'

MPs, Humphrys believes, can be divided into two groups: the principled type, who attempt to tell the truth and remain marooned on the backbenches; and the ministers, who have to tell lies. And he's absolutely right. As one cabinet minister has privately admitted to me, the collective responsibility for government policy that all ministers must accept means that they often have to defend decisions which they don't agree with. And that means lying.

So it seemed a refreshing change when on 22 September 2005, local government minister David Miliband adopted a disarmingly honest approach to handling criticism of government policy. Appearing on the BBC's *Question Time*, he was responding to the suggestion that Labour's decision to delay a review of local government spending was an 'apparent U-turn'.

> This isn't an apparent U-turn, this is a vaulting, 180 degrees full U-turn. I'm happy to come on this programme and say: 'Be in no doubt it's a U-turn ... let's be absolutely clear about that. There is nothing apparent about it.'

Miliband seemed in danger of giving politicians a good name. Or were his uncommonly frank remarks just a different kind of deception? The American newspaper columnist Michael Kinsley once observed that in US politics 'a gaffe is when a politician tells the truth'. But increasingly, in the UK at least, the very selective telling of the truth has become a subtle political tool. The late Mo Mowlam set the trend with her admission in 2000 that she had not only smoked cannabis, she had actually inhaled. Her confession, made after taking responsibility for the government's anti-drugs policy, enabled her to keep her job, and enhanced her reputation.

The astute politician can use the honesty ploy to great effect. An admission of a minor error or failure can suggest integrity and throw critics off the scent. 'Yes, I have to admit I am wearing odd socks, but I have no plans to raise taxes.' That sort of thing. And we'll take a close look at that weaselly phrase 'no plans to' in a minute.

Psychological magician Derren Brown offers an insight into just how clever and slippery politicians can be with language. For his television series he succeeded in getting a teller at a race-track to pay out on a losing betting ticket, by banging on the window and then insisting, against all reason, that the ticket was, in fact, a winning one. This was possible, he told me, because the girl had been repeating the same task countless times, and it had become automatic. Interrupting the process, by banging on the glass, confused her and made her open to suggestion. Telling her the ticket was a winning one offered her brain a route out of her confusion.

Why am I telling you this? Because politicians, Brown suggests, adopt a similar technique in order to get people to believe their lies and deceptions. What they do, he says, is confuse you with statistics and lull you into a suggestible state, and then offer you a way out, a simple proposition which you will be strongly inclined to accept. Margaret Thatcher, he says, used this method all the time. Well, after several minutes on the complex iniquities of past rating systems, who wouldn't welcome a nice simple community charge? Poll tax? Marvellous idea.

Falling short of the Washington standard

George Washington, the United States' first president, is held by most flag-waving Americans to have been a paragon of virtue and honesty – as illustrated in the famous story from his childhood as recorded by his biographer, Parson Mason Locke Weems:

> *George*, said his father, *do you know who killed that beautiful little cherry-tree yonder in the garden?* This was a *tough question*; and George staggered under it for a moment; but quickly recovered himself: and looking at his father, with the sweet face of youth brightened with the inexpressible charm of all-conquering truth, he bravely cried out, *'I can't tell a lie, Pa; you know I can't tell a lie. I did cut it with my hatchet.'* — *Run to my arms, you dearest boy*, cried his father in transports, *run to my arms; glad am I, George, that you killed my tree; for you have paid me for it a thousand fold. Such an act of heroism in my son, is more worth than a thousand trees, though blossomed with silver, and their fruits of purest gold.*

This, Weems suggests, shows the honourable and honest character of America's founding father. The problem is that the story is complete fiction – a lie. According to historian Karal Ann Marling, Weems was struggling to 'flesh out a believable and interesting figure, to humanise Washington', who had been painted as cold and colourless in an earlier biography.

Abraham Lincoln, incidentally, said that he didn't have a

good enough memory to be a liar. A good memory does seem to be an important facility for the habitual political liar, but a thick skin and flexible moral standards are probably more important.

It's said that Washington couldn't lie, Nixon couldn't tell the truth and Reagan didn't know the difference. The bit about Nixon certainly seems right.

> When I first learned from news reports about the Watergate break-in, I was appalled at this senseless, illegal action ... We must maintain integrity in the White House. There can be no White Wash in the White House ... No one in the White House staff, no one in this administration presently employed was involved in this very bizarre incident.

Richard 'Tricky Dicky' Nixon, one of the great political liars of all time, might have got away with it if he hadn't perspired so much. His sweatiness was a dead giveaway. It was considered a factor in preventing him from winning the presidency against Kennedy in 1960, and, arguably, it lost him the presidency in 1974 when two *Washington Post* reporters asked themselves: 'Why is that man sweating so much? Could it be, perhaps, that he is lying?'

> I want to say one thing to the American people – want you to listen to me – I'm going to say this again. I did not have sexual relations with that woman – Miss Lewinsky – I never told anybody to lie – not a single time. Never.

Bill Clinton's charm, apparent sincerity and flashing white teeth helped him survive, where others like Nixon had sweatily failed. Clinton was, according to psychologist Paul Ekman, technically a very poor liar. It was his use of 'distancing language', specifically his reference to Monica Lewinsky as 'that woman', which gave the game away. Professor Ekman compares it to that of an Australian husband whose wife had been murdered. The man went on television asking the public for help in 'this matter'. 'Of course he killed her', says Ekman.

He is convinced that Clinton wanted to be caught. 'Why did he pick on Lewinsky?', he asks. 'Because he wanted to be caught ... and to be loved anyhow.' Nixon, he believes, lied because he thought he was entitled to do so.

Ekman says that both Clinton and Nixon were 'ghastly' liars. For quality lying he singles out the performances of President Kennedy and the Soviet foreign minister Andrei Gromyko during the Cuban missile crisis in 1962. In their meetings, Gromyko was concealing the fact that his country had placed missiles in Cuba, and Kennedy was concealing the fact that he knew they had placed missiles in Cuba. Ekman says they were both 'inventive and clever in fabricating, smooth talkers, with a convincing manner.' But the pair very nearly lied their way into World War III.

George W. Bush has inherited the mantle of a long line of lying presidents, and the signs are that he's trying hard to live up to their standard, rather than that set by that other George W. – America's first president.

This is, at least, the opinion of the not-entirely-unbiased Washington editor of *The Nation* magazine, David Corn, who notes that Bush came to power in 2000 as a candidate who 'could restore honour and integrity to an Oval Office stained by the misdeeds and falsehoods of his predecessor.' Writing in 2003, Corn said: 'George W. Bush is a liar. He has lied large and small, directly and by omission. Through his campaign for the presidency and his first years in the White House, he has mugged the truth – not merely in honest error, but deliberately, consistently, and repeatedly to advance his career and agenda.'

There is a fair amount of consensus across the political spectrum that Bush, at the very least, exaggerated the threat from Iraq as an excuse for going to war. His assertions that Saddam Hussein possessed 'a massive stockpile' of unconventional weapons and was dealing directly with Al-Qaeda have never been substantiated. Nor were his earlier claims that Iraq was 'six months away' from developing a nuclear weapon.

Magazine articles and a whole raft of books have catalogued the lies and distortions allegedly perpetrated by the world's most powerful man. Bush-baiting has become big business. In 2004, film-maker Michael Moore's award-winning documentary *Fahrenheit 9/11* portrayed the President as an incompetent fool who took the US to war in Iraq on a lie. The film did phenomenal business at the box office around the world, but conspicuously failed to achieve its stated objective – to prevent George W. Bush from being re-elected. As was subsequently echoed in Britain, the electorate decided that if it had been lied to about the reasons for being taken to war, it was prepared to forgive. Ultimately, it seems, the public will tolerate almost any amount of lies – as long as the economy is strong.

* * *

And by the way, politicians' wives can also be guilty of bending the truth. Nancy Reagan routinely lied about her age, usually deducting two years from reality. College and high school records indicate her date of birth as 1921. White House staff were, however, instructed to tell the media that she was born in 1923. In 1988 she had a much-publicised party at the White House to celebrate her 65th birthday. She was, in fact, 67.

Not to be outdone

One of the most spectacular bare-faced lies in modern British politics occurred back in March 1963, when Secretary of State for War John Profumo stood up in the House of Commons and said that there had been 'no impropriety whatsoever' in his relationship with the model and showgirl Christine Keeler. Profumo was in fact having a passionate affair with Keeler – a scenario made even more compromising by the fact that she had also been sleeping with Eugene Ivanov, the naval attaché at the Soviet embassy.

Just ten weeks after his Commons denial, Profumo was again addressing MPs, this time saying 'with deep remorse' that he had misled the House and would resign.

Several decades later, another darling of the Conservative Party tumbled from grace after being exposed as a liar. We have already established that Jeffrey Archer could not be relied upon to fill in his CV honestly, but that was to be just a taste of the deception to come during a career which saw him become an MP, Tory deputy chairman and a peer. Alongside his career in politics he was making millions as a purveyor of fiction, but somewhere along the line the two strands of his life seem to have become muddled.

Archer once told me that he harboured no delusion that he was a great writer. He then rather spoiled it by adding grandly that someone had once likened his work to that of Somerset Maugham. His initial modesty, of course, was a deception.

Anyway, in 1999, Tory leader William Hague described Archer (despite a lot of circumstantial evidence to the contrary) as a person of 'probity and of integrity'. This was by way of explaining his party's surprising decision to make him its candidate for Mayor of London. Hague had to eat his words shortly afterwards when Archer was charged with perjury and perverting the course of justice. The ennobled author was sentenced to four years in prison after a jury decided he had lied under oath during his 1987 libel case against the *Daily Star* which alleged that he had had sex with the prostitute Monica Coghlan.

Hague blamed his misjudgment on 'false assurances' he'd been given by Archer. The Tory leader didn't last much longer himself. But why on earth had Hague been so trusting in the first place?

Jeffrey Archer's biographer Michael Crick reveals that the schoolboy Jeffrey once dived into a swimming pool and cracked his head on the bottom. 'After which he was never the same', he observes. Perhaps all politicians have, in their earlier lives, received a severe bang on the head.

A dishonourable mention must also be made of Jonathan Aitken, who, like Archer, made the mistake of lying under oath. The Tory defence procurement minister's downfall followed newspaper allegations that, while responsible for a big Middle East defence deal, he had spent a weekend at the Ritz Hotel in Paris, paid for by a Saudi businessman involved in the transaction. Aitken decided to tackle his accusers head on:

> If it now falls to me to start a fight to cut out the cancer of bent and twisted journalism in our country with the sword of truth and the trusty shield of traditional British fair play ... so be it. I am ready for that fight. The fight against falsehood and all who peddle it.

But after the collapse of his libel action against *The Guardian* and Granada TV, Aitken's lies were exposed. In June 1999, the man tipped as a potential future prime minister was jailed for eighteen months after he pleaded guilty to charges of perjury and conspiracy to pervert the course of justice.

In sentencing him, Mr Justice Scott Baker said: 'For nearly four years you wove a web of deceit in which you entangled yourself and from which there was no way out unless you were prepared to come clean and tell the truth. Unfortunately you were not.'

The former minister had compounded his deceitfulness by trying to get his daughter to falsely testify that she had been the occupant of the Ritz hotel room. In the end it was Aitken who was impaled on the 'sword of truth'.

We have, so far, no real equivalent to Watergate. No British Prime Minister has yet been forced to resign after lying to the public. Lies – or alleged lies – did, however, force a Labour transport secretary to step down from office in May 2002, after a mauling by the press.

Liar Byers ... pants on fire.

Daily Mail

Consider Matilda, the little girl in Hilaire Belloc's *Cautionary Tales*. Matilda, you will recall, used to summon the fire brigade frivolously, so ensuring that, when there really was a fire, no one believed her. Thus it is with Stephen Byers. We cannot be sure whom to believe.

Evening Standard

Spinocchio: The lie keeps growing and growing ... until it's as clear as the nose on your face.

Daily Telegraph

Stephen Byers's troubles began after the leaking of the infamous memo by Jo Moore, a special adviser to his department, in which she suggested that September 11 2001 would be 'a good day' to bury bad news on transport figures.

It sparked months of infighting within the transport department, and involved the communications director, former BBC correspondent Martin Sixsmith. The press and opposition MPs accused Byers of lying to Parliament when he announced that Sixsmith had resigned, when in fact he had not. It compounded earlier claims that he had misled MPs over his decision to put Railtrack into administration.

In announcing his resignation, Byers said that he was going in order to avoid causing further damage to the government. He 'regretted any confusion', but said he had 'behaved honourably'. He added: 'People who know me best know I am not a liar.'

But three years later, in July 2005, Byers was forced to admit in the High Court that he had not been truthful to MPs about the events leading up to Railtrack's collapse.

During a compensation case brought by Railtrack shareholders, the former minister was challenged over a Commons statement he'd made about when the Railtrack administration proposals had first been discussed. Under questioning, Byers admitted that his answer to MPs had been untrue, and that the prospect of a change in Railtrack's status had, in fact, been discussed earlier than he had admitted.

Asked if this had been 'deliberately not an accurate statement', Byers replied: 'It was such a long time ago, I cannot remember, but it is not a truthful statement and I apologise for that. I cannot remember the motives behind it.'

You may need to have a good memory to be a good liar – but a bad memory can be useful if you are rumbled.

But can a politician recover from the political embarrassment of being caught in a lie? Byers's Labour colleague Beverly Hughes resigned as immigration minister in April 2004 after 'unwittingly' misleading people about lax visa checks on Romanian and Bulgarian immigrants. She told reporters that she was not aware of the problem, but it later emerged that she had been warned about it by colleagues a year earlier. In Tony Blair's post-election cabinet reshuffle just over a year later she returned to government as children's minister. All forgiven and forgotten.

* * *

The first casualty of war

In what sense was the Iraq War a war? Wars are normally fought between nations in situations where the outcome is not a foregone conclusion. Conflicts in which one side massively out-guns the other are, surely, something else. In the view of Terry Jones in *The Observer*:

> Dropping bombs from a safe height on an already hard-pressed people, whose infrastructure is in chaos from years of sanctions and who live under an oppressive regime, isn't a 'war'. It's a turkey shoot.

He also questions the language used by both Bush and Blair in describing their joint commitment to the 'war on terrorism'.

> You can wage war against another country, or on a national group within your own country, but you can't wage war on an abstract noun. How do you know when you've won? When you've got it removed from the *Oxford English Dictionary*?

But it sounds good, doesn't it? Waging a war against terrorism. Our governments aren't just stepping up security and other counter-terrorist measures, they are actually going to war against terrorism. Enormously comforting. Will it be over by Christmas?

The terrorists are themselves equally adept at distorting language for their own purposes. We grew accustomed over the years to paramilitary organisations in Northern Ireland referring to the 'legitimate targets' of their bombs and bullets – even though a victim may have been guilty of nothing more than delivering milk to an army base. And, extraordinarily, they will 'claim responsibility' for the cold-blooded murder of a defenceless man in front of his wife and children, as if they deserve some sort of prize.

We have also become familiar with the way language is used politically to soften and sanitise the terrible realities of war. 'Degrading enemy forces' doesn't mean debasing and demeaning them. That, of course, happens to prisoners of war after the conflict. During the first Gulf War, a US military spokesman said that allied forces had 'degraded by 70 per cent' a body of Iraqi soldiers. They had, of course, killed nearly three-quarters of them.

Other examples include:

- Render non-viable – means kill people
- Collateral damage – means dead people
- Armed reconnaissance – means bombing the enemy
- Servicing the target – means bombing the enemy
- Accidental delivery of ordnance – means bombing your own troops
- Friendly fire – means bombing your own troops
- Going home in a body bag – unfortunately, means going home in a body bag

Even torture has its euphemisms. In some military circles it's disingenuously referred to as 'enhanced interrogation techniques'. But deception in wartime is not just about euphemism; it also involves outright lies. And it's by no means a modern phenomenon.

During the First World War there were many reports of German atrocities in Belgium and France, and in order to establish the truth about these rumours, the British government set up an investigating committee under the chairmanship of Lord Bryce. The report, issued in 1915, was full of harrowing, graphic tales of summary executions, torture, rape, families burned alive and babies speared on bayonets. In fact it was almost entirely invented; there was almost no evidence for the majority of the gruesome stories. The historian H.C. Peterson called the Bryce Report 'one of the worst atrocities of the war'.

Among the most blatant lies of the 20th century was that told by Adolf Hitler to Neville Chamberlain – that he had no further military ambitions in Europe. Chamberlain returned to Britain believing that he had achieved 'peace in our time'. He even wrote to his sister that Hitler was 'a man who could be relied upon when he had given his word'. Hitler's lie bought him crucial extra time to prepare his army for the invasion of Czechoslovakia.

Psychologist Paul Ekman believes that Hitler's deceit succeeded partly because he was an accomplished liar and partly because Chamberlain was receptive to deception. 'Chamberlain was not a dumb man', says Ekman. 'But he wanted to believe Hitler. He had staked his country's future on his ability to negotiate with that man.'

Hitler's skill at lying was shared by his propaganda chief Joseph Goebbels, who dressed up his government's genocidal extermination of millions of Jews as its 'relocation' policy. Goebbels famously asserted that 'if you tell a lie big enough and keep repeating it, people will eventually come to believe it.' And if they didn't, they could always be relocated.

Inspiration for the Nazis' 'Final Solution' seems to have come from the Ottoman Empire's slaughter of more than a million Armenians during the First World War. Forced death marches and systematic mass executions took place under the cover of a government policy of 'deportation'. Hitler, in giving orders for the 'merciless' killing of men, women and children during the invasion of Poland, wrote: 'Who, after all, speaks today of the annihilation of the Armenians?'

The Armenian slaughter, now widely recognised as the first genocide of the 20th century, is still denied by Turkey. In 2004 a spokesman from the Turkish Embassy in London said:

> Some parts of the Armenian population became instrumental to Tsarist Russia's expansion strategy and established armed bands to stage a guerrilla war behind the Ottoman battle lines. The Ottoman government's resulting decision to displace them out of the war zone caused losses both from the Armenian and the local Muslim (Turkish) population. This was not a policy of extermination or genocide.

Which doesn't exactly explain the death of more than a million Armenians.

British politicians are not averse to relocating the truth in times of war. What else are we to make of government statements about the sinking of the Argentine cruiser *Belgrano* during the Falklands conflict? The British had declared a 200-mile 'exclusion zone' around the islands, and threatened to sink any Argentine naval vessels found inside.

On 2 April 1982, the *Belgrano* was sailing twenty miles outside the exclusion zone when it was sunk by a British submarine – with the loss of 368 lives. The attack was made with the full authority of the British Cabinet. Defence secretary John Nott said: 'This heavily armed surface attack group was close to the total exclusion zone and was closing on elements of our task force which was only hours away.' But subsequent evidence strongly suggested that the *Belgrano* had been travelling away from the task force when it was torpedoed.

During the Iraq war, many observers identified the 'incredible shrinking language' used by George Bush in particular to defend the military action. In March 2003, the war was about 'finding and destroying Saddam Hussein's weapons of mass destruction'. Three months later, Bush was talking about 'weapons of mass destruction programmes'. By October they had become 'weapons of mass destruction-related programmes'. In January 2004 we had gone to war because of 'weapons of mass destruction-related programmes activities'.

The truth is indeed the first casualty of war. It's going home in a body bag.

Political English

Political language is designed to make lies sound truthful and murder respectable, and to give an appearance of solidity to pure wind.

George Orwell, 'Politics and the English Language'

Politicians over the years have developed their own unique style of English; a sort of self-defence language which gets them out of tight spots, avoids accountability, rewrites history and generally circumvents the truth.

Four years after he resigned as President for his part in covering up the Watergate scandal, Richard Nixon explained:

'I was not lying. I said things that later on seemed to be untrue.' Other classic examples include:

I wasn't lying, Senator, I was presenting a different version from the facts.

Oliver North

It depends upon what the meaning of the word 'is' is.

Bill Clinton

That's not a lie, it's a terminological inexactitude.

US Secretary of State Alexander Haig

But one of the most extraordinary pieces of sustained political-speak came not from an elected politician but from a civil servant. The evidence given by British Cabinet secretary Sir Robert Armstrong at the 'Spycatcher' trial in 1986 is a delicious example of what can happen when someone from the world of politics realises that he's running out of ways to avoid telling the truth.

The British government was taking legal action in the Australian courts, trying to prevent publication of former MI5 agent Peter Wright's book, *Spycatcher*, revealing secrets of how the service worked. It resulted in a remarkable courtroom exchange between Wright's counsel, Malcolm Turnbull, and Sir Robert.

Turnbull was trying to establish whether Sir Robert Armstrong had been entirely honest when he wrote to Mr William Armstrong, chairman of Wright's publishers, Sidgwick and Jackson, asking for two copies of his book, leaving the clear, but possibly false, impression that the British government did not yet have a copy and was not aware of its contents.

TURNBULL: That letter was calculated to mislead, was it not?

ARMSTRONG: It was calculated to ask for a copy of the book on which we could take direct action.

TURNBULL: It was calculated to mislead Mr Armstrong to believe that the government did not have a copy of the book. Correct?

ARMSTRONG: It was calculated not to disclose to Mr Armstrong that the government had a copy of the book in order to protect the confidentiality of the source from which it came ...

Later:

TURNBULL: You said to His Honour a little while ago that you could not remember an occasion when you had been placed in the unhappy circumstance of having to misrepresent the facts or to lie in order to protect the sources of MI5 or national security?

ARMSTRONG: I think I said that I had not been in a position where I had to tell an untruth. I think that was the nature of the question I answered.

TURNBULL: The letter is an untruth, is it not?

ARMSTRONG: It is what I have said. It was designed to protect the confidentiality of the source and to avoid the disclosure that a copy of the book had been obtained.

TURNBULL: Sir Robert ...

ARMSTRONG: If that is misrepresenting, yes it was.

TURNBULL: Do you understand the difference between a truth and an untruth?

ARMSTRONG: I hope so.

... and later still:

TURNBULL: You conveyed to [the publishers] the clear impression that you did not already have a copy of the book, did you not?

ARMSTRONG: Yes, I did, because I was wishing to protect the confidentiality of the source from which we had obtained it.

TURNBULL: And that impression was not a true impression, was it?

ARMSTRONG: Well, clearly we had a copy of the book.

TURNBULL: So it contains a lie.

ARMSTRONG: It was a misleading impression. It does not contain a lie, I don't think.

TURNBULL: What is the difference between a misleading impression and a lie?

ARMSTRONG: A lie is a straight untruth.

TURNBULL: What is a misleading impression – a sort of bent untruth?

ARMSTRONG: As one person said, it is perhaps being economical with the truth.

Armstrong's comment, intended almost certainly as a little joke, stunned the courtroom, electrified the world's press and introduced a new phrase into public parlance. It was now OK to deceive and dissemble. It wasn't lying any more, just being *economical with the truth*.

* * *

Politicians are also masters of exploiting the loopholes in language.

If a politician is asked if he is going to do something – raise taxes, resign, call a General Election, declare war or whatever – in many instances he will reply that he has 'no plans to do so'.

This, of course, means precisely nothing. He may have every intention of doing any of those things, but if he is not in possession of a typed and bound document spelling out the details, he can legitimately say he has 'no plans' to do so.

And what, for example, was the absolute truth when, after the Iraq War, British defence secretary Geoff Hoon said the government had 'no plans to send an extra 1,300 troops' to join the peace-keeping force? In reality, the government might have been planning to send 1,200 troops or 1,400 troops, but Hoon's statement would still have been technically truthful. In the event, of course, many more troops would be sent to Iraq on various occasions over the following years, though never in a contingent of precisely 1,300.

Politicians also love the word 'committed'. They will declare that they are 'committed to establishing a fairer society' or 'committed to improving public services'. Why don't they just come out and say they 'will' do these things? Presumably this would sound too much like a promise, and therefore be much harder to renege on.

Tony Blair once declared that he was 'committed to the future of Africa'. Word-watcher Don Watson believes that he might just as well have said: 'Why don't I just look in the general direction of Nairobi and wave?' It would mean as much.

John Humphrys, in his book *Lost For Words*, exempts at least one politician from any accusation of being devious with language. It's the man responsible for regaling the House of Commons with the following curious observation:

> I think, as the Right Honourable Member made clear in the debate on Monday, the judgement about President Reagan, I must say on my part whatever was said about President Reagan, and there was, I must say that in fact

whatever they said about at the beginning of his regime, he did contribute to reducing the weapons of mass destruction and I think that was a contribution to the world peace.

Deputy Prime Minister John Prescott has never been much of a wordsmith. John Humphrys suggests that the veteran politician's difficulties with language have meant that he has never mastered the art of concealment or, by extension, manipulation. 'When you hear him speak without a script, you hear him think.'

Alas, there's only one John Prescott.

* * *

We place a lot of trust in our politicians. We give them around a third of everything we earn, and trust them to spend it wisely. We trust them to make decisions affecting almost every aspect of our lives – our health, our children's education, our defence against evil dictators with weapons of mass destruction.

At election time we choose which politicians we trust the most. Which candidate do we think seems most honest and sincere? Unfortunately, the majority of politicians seem to subscribe to the Groucho Marx philosophy that 'the secret of success is sincerity. Once you can fake that, you've got it made.' And most politicians have a greater command of language than John Prescott, and therefore a well-developed ability to deceive.

All we can do is put a cross in a box and hope. Politicians are, after all, just like you and me, doing what comes naturally – lying their way through life. Just as we all play the role of businesspeople at certain times in our lives, so too are we politicians. We are all adept at making promises we never intend to keep and are perfectly capable of contorting an argument to win a point or to get our own way. And we certainly know how to deny responsibility or to blame someone else when things go wrong. We are indeed the Right Honourable Members for our own personal constituencies.

And before anyone is tempted to punish their child for lying about eating a chocolate biscuit, remember, he or she may simply be practising the skills needed to take the country to war.

CHAPTER SEVEN

A bad press?

Most people think journalists are liars. And that's official.

For more than twenty years, MORI has been running a survey to find out who the British public trust to tell the truth. Journalists consistently fare badly, lagging woefully behind more trusted professionals such as doctors, teachers and clergymen. In 2003, journalists tied for bottom place with politicians. Since then they have come last all on their own. In 2005, only 16 per cent of the public indicated any faith in them. Four out of five people don't believe what journalists say.

As if trying to prove the public right about journalists, the *Financial Times* found a remarkable way of reporting the 2003 poll results. It ran the headline: 'Business leaders enjoy revival in public trust', based on businessmen improving a statistically insignificant 3 per cent, from 25 to 28 per cent, over the previous year. An astonished Robert M. Worcester, chairman of MORI, said: 'If the *Financial Times* does this to make their readers feel good, then little wonder that journalists rate bottom of the poll for their veracity.' And he added, pointedly: 'And the FT is thought generally to be the best of the lot.'

Journalists, however, did fare better in an international poll commissioned by the BBC World Service in 2005. Religious leaders came out best, trusted by 33 per cent of the 50,000 people interviewed in 68 countries. Politicians came firmly bottom, trusted by just 13 per cent. Journalists came somewhere in the middle on 26 per cent, though, significantly, they were particularly distrusted in Europe.

How can it be that journalists, members of a profession with such a long and noble tradition of exposing misdeeds and righting wrongs, whose role is to provide the facts, to inform and to communicate, have become so distrusted? It's certainly nothing new. Journalists would probably have fared little better in a poll 100 years ago when, in America, William Randolph Hearst and Joseph Pulitzer more or less invented the art of sensationalist reporting. In the circulation war between Hearst's *New York Journal* and Pulitzer's *World*, both men were prepared to fabricate stories to gain an edge over the other. Public concern about Spanish colonial rule in neighbouring Cuba provided fertile territory, prompting lurid headlines such as 'Spanish Cannibalism', 'Inhuman Torture' and 'Amazon Warriors Fight for Rebels'.

In 1897, convinced that a war was imminent between Spain and America, Hearst sent the artist and correspondent Frederick Remington to Cuba to investigate. The following cablegrams were, allegedly, exchanged:

> Everything is quiet. There is no trouble here. There will be no war. I wish to return. *Remington*

> Please remain. You furnish the pictures and I'll furnish the war. *W.R. Hearst*

This famous correspondence may itself be a fiction (there's no proof of its existence), but it certainly reflects the newspaper tycoon's intention. The following year, Hearst got his war – a conflict at least partly forced on the US government by the anti-Spanish sentiment stirred up by his fabricated stories.

The tradition of journalistic invention, of not letting the facts get in the way of a good story, has been kept ingloriously alive over the years, driven often to ludicrous ends, as demonstrated spectacularly in this article in the May 2005 edition of *Weekly World News*.

CONFEDERACY WAS BUILDING AN ATOMIC BOMB ... 80 YEARS BEFORE WW2!

Civil War historians are reeling over the discovery that a Confederate scientist was just weeks away from perfecting a crude atomic bomb – and planned to use the device to destroy Washington, DC, 138 years ago ... in 1864!

Physicist Thaddeus McMullen was killed before he could carry out the plot, reveals Joel Remarsh, a Civil War historian who uncovered McMullen's maniacal plan while studying a collection of war-era journals, letters and documents given to him by McMullen's descendants.

'My blood ran cold when I realized what I was reading', says Remarsh, who plans to reveal all in a book tentatively titled *Southern Victory: The Confederacy's Atomic War*.

This startling revelation came quite close on the heels of another *Weekly World News* front-page exclusive: 'Alien Skulls Found On Mars.' The publication operates in a tough market-place, competing with rival 'newspapers' staffed by intrepid reporters capable of uncovering some remarkable stories:

VEGGIE-EATING MOTHER HAS GREEN BABY!

GUST OF WIND BLOWS MIDGET BALLOON PEDDLER 20 MILES

MISSING BABY FOUND INSIDE WATERMELON! HE'S ALIVE!

2000-YEAR-OLD MAN FOUND IN TREE ... WEARING WATCH THAT STILL TICKS!

EGYPTIAN MUMMY IS FATHER OF MY CHILD

FLEA CIRCUS GOES WILD WITH HUNGER AND ATTACKS TRAINER!

Few, if any, of the journals involved could be even remotely described as genuine newspapers, though they are often read as if they were. Despite claims to be a legitimate newspaper, Britain's *Daily Sport* is still happy to regale readers with tales such as the classic 'WW2 Bomber Found On The Moon', illustrated by a picture of the moon with a plane superimposed on it. Shortly afterwards, the *Sport* published a photo of just the moon, with the caption 'WW2 Bomber Found On Moon VANISHES'.

And the *News of the World*, Britain's best-selling Sunday newspaper, unashamedly dedicated an entire front page back in October 1983 to the story 'UFO LANDS IN SUFFOLK – and that's official'. At least the UFO story was a distraction from the *News of the World*'s usual fare of dubious celebrity gossip, tales of torrid three-in-a-bed sex and salacious stories of vicars running away with Sunday school teachers. What next? 'Alien took me to heaven and back – says Suffolk girl.'

These kinds of stories are just one style of journalistic fiction – arguably, given their transparency, the least damaging.

It's the more sophisticated lies, distortions and inventions which permeate a great deal of modern journalism that need to be identified and challenged. Of course journalists tell lies (they're human, after all); the question is when, if at all, are we to believe them? The answer, according to some at least, is never.

Aneurin Bevan said that he read papers avidly. 'It's my one form of continuous fiction', he explained. Poet and man of letters Humbert Wolfe was equally cynical:

> You cannot hope
> to bribe or twist
> thank God! the
> British journalist.
>
> But, seeing what
> the man will do
> unbribed, there's
> no occasion to.

Scepticism of the outpourings of the press is healthy and to be encouraged. But in the opinion of some, journalists are the devil incarnate. Among their most vociferous critics, ironically, are the politicians with whom, as we shall see, they have such a strong interdependent relationship. Other haters of the press include the Royal family – all members, without exception – and almost anyone who has, fairly or unfairly, been exposed, pilloried or simply criticised in the newspapers or on the radio or television. This latter group includes celebrities, who, like politicians, rely on the press for exposure but do not hesitate to scream 'liar' when the relationship turns sour.

Public confidence in journalism is currently lower than ever. Newspapers, competing against radio, television and the internet, are in steep decline – and desperate to gain advantage over each other. Circulation wars, as in the days of Hearst and Pulitzer, are never good for journalistic veracity. When you add to this the other factors which can lead to bad journalism – incompetence, laziness, prejudice, political bias and personal ambition – you start to comprehend the size of the problem.

Lies, damned lies and the press

Most newspaper 'inaccuracies' go undetected, or at least un-challenged. But those who fall victim to them, and decide to do something about it, have recourse in the UK to a 'fast, free and fair' service, provided by the Press Complaints Commission.

PCC investigations are carried out under a voluntary code of practice, drawn up by and subscribed to by the vast majority of British newspapers. Editors are bound, at least in theory, by its decisions, which usually require them to publish corrections or apologies.

In 2002, for example, the PPC investigated a complaint arising from a story in the *Sunday Sport* which revealed 'a night of sex' involving Coronation Street actor Jimmi Harkishin, who played a character called Dev Alahan, and a woman he had met in a nightclub. Under the headline 'Corrie Jimmi is a Dev-il in bed!', it gave details of the woman's version of events.

The actor told the PCC investigators that he had met the woman once, in the nightclub, but that he had rejected her suggestion that they leave together. He complained that the *Sunday Sport* had not asked him if the story was true.

It is not the PCC's job, nor is it within its power, to establish 'the truth' in this kind of case. Its role is to decide if the newspaper was in a position to know what the truth was. In this case it decided that the *Sunday Sport* was not in possession of any evidence to support the woman's version of events, and that the newspaper should have approached the actor for corroboration. The Commission upheld Harkishin's complaint, concluding that the *Sunday Sport* had 'failed to take sufficient care to avoid publishing inaccurate material'.

Another case investigated by the PPC involved the footballer Stan Collymore, who complained that *The Sun*, in accusing him of lying, had itself been dishonest.

Two days after Collymore attracted publicity with his allegations that had been beaten up in Dublin by several rugby players, *The Sun* published an article trailed on the front page with the headline 'I lied: Stan Collymore's sensational signed confession to the Sun.'

The reality, asserted Collymore, was that the newspaper had got one of its Page Three girls to ask for his autograph at a book-signing session. The 'confession' was on the piece of paper he signed. The rather significant detail that the 'sensational signed confession' was a mere scam was revealed only in the text of the article – printed on an inside page. The PPC upheld the complaint on the grounds that the newspaper had 'failed to take sufficient care to highlight the way in which the confession had been obtained.'

It's deeply worrying that Britain's best-selling newspaper, with the reputed power to sway General Election results, could resort to such low and deceptive tactics to get a story. All things, it seems, are fair in love and circulation war.

What can be done to stop newspapers behaving in this way? The PCC can't impose fines, though it doesn't actually think it would achieve much if it could. The Commission argues that editors are more deterred by the prospect of having to apologise in their own papers than by the threat of a fine, which anyway would be unlikely to come out of their own pockets.

The PCC received 3,649 complaints in 2003 – by no means

all from celebrities or other high-profile figures. Of the complaints, approximately four out of ten were about inaccurate reporting. Many cases were resolved without the need for an adjudication. In cases where a PCC verdict was required, around 45 per cent of the complaints were upheld. But how many aggrieved victims of unfair, distorted or deceitful reporting never lodge complaints? *The Sun* should investigate.

* * *

Victims of journalists' 'lies' do, of course, have the protection of libel laws and can seek financial redress in the courts. But it can be a high-risk tactic in the UK, as legal aid isn't available in libel cases. This gives wealthy newspapers a huge advantage over less affluent victims of their inaccurate and defamatory reporting. In taking decisions about publication, newspapers will often give as much attention to the likelihood that someone will sue, as to any consideration of truth and accuracy. They know that many people will be deterred from taking legal action by the tremendous financial consequences of losing.

Conversely, broadsheet editors with less money in the bank than their red top rivals complain that their attempts to expose criminal misbehaviour are often thwarted by rich litigants who, like Robert Maxwell in the past, shower them with menacing injunctions. Reporters trying to expose a complex fraud, for example, know that if they make a small mistake, it could cost their employers hundreds of thousands of pounds in damages and costs. But the tabloid newspapers are not so inhibited; their relentless pursuit of celebrity gossip and sensation often leads them to step over the mark, and into the libel courts.

In 1998, Hollywood actor Tom Cruise and his then wife Nicole Kidman won substantial undisclosed damages in their case against Express Newspapers over an article which alleged that their marriage was a sham designed to cover up their homosexuality. It claimed that Cruise was impotent and sterile.

What journalistic lengths might we suppose the *Express* went to in order to substantiate the accuracy of its story before going to print? Did it have medical evidence of the actor's sterility? Had it spoken to either partner? No, it had based its story on a series of unfounded rumours and had, presumably, calculated that the benefits of running its dubious 'scoop' would outweigh the financial risks of being sued.

Cruise and Kidman are among many celebrities who have fought the tabloids and won. But the newspapers don't always get it wrong. Jeffrey Archer, as we've established, had to pay back the £500,000 he received after suing the *Daily Star* over the Monica Coghlan allegations. But that returned half-a-million pounds is but a drop in the ocean compared to the mountains of cash paid out by British newspapers as a consequence of their badly researched and often mendacious stories.

Bad boys of journalism

Newspaper lies can be generated by unscrupulous reporters who either don't believe, or choose to conveniently forget, that the basic ethics of the profession apply to them. Facts, they believe, are for journalists with the time, energy and patience to concern themselves with such tiresome things. These bad boys of journalism see reporting as a game of *Blankety Blank* in which they are required to use their vivid imaginations to fill in the missing words.

Principled journalists have been taken to court, even sent to prison for refusing to 'reveal their sources', not prepared to compromise the people who have tipped them off. In July 2005, *New York Times* journalist Judith Millar was jailed for four months for contempt after refusing to reveal her source in an investigation into the unmasking of an undercover CIA agent. Less scrupulous journalists are more likely to refuse to reveal their sources because they don't have any.

Back in the 1970s I came across a local newspaper reporter in the Midlands who practised *Blankety Blank* journalism and wasn't ashamed to admit it. He was typing up a report about local residents 'up in arms' over chronic damp in their council flats. Rather than visit the flats to assess the situation, he was simply making up the quotes. 'It's disgusting'; 'There's green mould all over my bedroom ceiling'; 'It's damaging the health of my children'; 'The council has got to do something about it.' Attempting to justify his behaviour, he said he had covered many similar stories in the past and people always said the same thing. What was the point in leaving his nice warm office?

He was not the first, nor the last journalist to plump for fiction over fact. In December 2003, *The People* newspaper sacked reporter Stewart Fowler and photographer David New for faking a picture used to illustrate a story about drugs being sold outside schools. The article, headlined 'On sale at school gates ... kiddie coke at 50p a go', claimed that drug dealers were offering the stimulant Ritalin to children as young as eight. It described how the paper had gone undercover to make contact with a dealer called Rev – 'a surly 19-year-old from Bow, east London, dressed in ripped jeans and a leather jacket, with short black spiky hair'. The accompanying photograph of the drug dealer outside school gates was, in fact, New's son.

New and Fowler subsequently sued Mirror Group Newspapers for unfair dismissal, claiming they had been ordered to fake the picture. The company eventually agreed to pay an undisclosed sum to its two former employees – and we are left to draw our own conclusions about who, if anyone, was telling the truth there.

Allegedly faked photographs of the abuse by British soldiers of Iraqi prisoners cost *Daily Mail* editor Piers Morgan his job in May 2004. Morgan argues that it has never been proved that the photographs he published were phony, but Bob Satchwell, Director of the Society of Editors, commented at the time that 'the lesson is to check, check and check again' and to 'always get it right'.

The credibility of the press in America is currently suffering the effects of a series of high-profile scandals involving over-imaginative reporters who have not been getting it right.

In February 2002, the *New York Times Magazine* reporter Michael Finkel was sacked after his story about child slavery in West Africa was exposed as a subtle blend of fact and fiction. He had taken a handful of interviews with different workers on a cocoa plantation and merged them to create one make-believe character. 'I thought I'd get away with it', he says. 'I was writing about impoverished, illiterate teenagers in the jungles of West Africa. Who would be able to determine that my main character didn't exist?' But his invention was spotted and his career brought to an abrupt conclusion.

US journalism is fuelled by a level of competitiveness unheard of in Britain. For the successful US reporter there is fame, fortune and the ultimate reward of a Pulitzer Prize. Think Lois Lane in *Superman*. But being caught cheating can bring ignominy.

A year after the Finkel case, another highly-respected *New York Times* reporter was discovered to have committed repeated 'acts of journalistic fraud', including stealing material from other papers and inventing quotes. Jayson Blair resigned after his own newspaper apologised for his 'widespread fabrications and plagiarism'. The *Times* said: 'Mr Blair repeatedly violated the cardinal tenet of journalism, which is simply truth.' His departure was followed rapidly by the resignations of editor Howell Raines and managing editor Gerald Boyd.

The next journalist to fall on his sword was five-times Pulitzer Prize nominee Jack Kelley, a star foreign correspondent on *USA Today*. The paper found strong evidence casting doubt on some of Kelley's stories, including a supposed eyewitness account of a suicide bombing in Jerusalem and his claim to have joined a high-speed hunt for Osama Bin Laden. Kelley resigned in January 2004 after admitting he had 'misled' the paper.

But one of the most high-profile cases of journalistic invention involved Stephen Glass, a rising star at the political and social commentary magazine *The New Republic*, whose story has since been turned into the Hollywood movie *Shattered Glass*.

Glass wrote dozens of articles for a number of national publications in which he simply made things up. There was a story about a political memorabilia convention featuring 'Monica Lewinsky condoms', and another about an evangelical church that worshipped George W. Bush. One article accused the former presidential advisor Vernon Jordan of behaving lecherously towards young women. Glass had invented his anonymous sources.

He developed cunning ways to subvert the efforts of the fact-checkers employed to vet stories for inaccuracies. 'I invented fake notes. I invented a series of voice mailboxes and business cards. I invented newsletters. I invented a website', says Glass. 'For every lie I told in the magazine, there was a series of lies behind that lie – in order to get it published.'

He was finally exposed when a magazine, trying to follow up one of his stories about a fifteen-year-old computer hacker, found it impossible to confirm a single fact.

It could never happen here – could it? And would we be surprised, or even care, if it did? It may well be that British journalists are just as capable, and as guilty, of such creative invention; it's just that as we don't have the same tradition of fact-checking, such aberrations go largely unidentified.

Watch your language

In a speech to a Society of Editors conference, the editor of BBC Radio's *Today* programme, Kevin Marsh, as part of a series of criticisms of journalistic standards in general, argued that 'a partial truth – in both senses of the word – is more lethal than a blatant untruth'.

We'll look at partial truth, in the sense of biased and prejudiced reporting, in a moment. Partial truth, meaning incomplete truth, covers a range of sins. At one end of the scale we're talking about gross misrepresentations of facts which fall just short of being outright lies – reporting selected information to present a politician or celebrity in a bad light, for example, or printing a quote out of context to convey, if possible, the opposite of what the speaker intended. Information and pictures can also be deliberately juxtaposed to create a misleading impression. These are not, technically, lies, but fall a long way short of the truth.

At the less serious end of the scale come clichés. Clichés are hardly serious deceptions, but they still get in the way of the whole truth. Clichés reduce news stories to ... well ... clichés. The subtleties that distinguish one story from another can get lost in the language of lazy journalism.

Over the many years I have worked with journalist and broadcaster John Humphrys, I have never known him slow to point out the clichés in my writing. In his recent book *Lost For Words*, John identifies some of his favourites from *other* sources:

- Feelings always run high
- Doubts are always nagging
- Warnings (and reminders) are always stark and the consequences of ignoring them are dire
- Reality is always grim
- Murders are always brutal (can a murder be gentle?) and all quarrels are bitter
- Daylight still reveals the charred remains
- Any house that is marginally more comfortable than a Calcutta slum is a luxury home – especially if it is owned by someone of whom the newspaper disapproves
- People die tragically (as opposed to joyfully)
- Famines are always Biblical

The problem is that this language doesn't reflect subtleties of meaning. Doubts described as 'nagging' may, in reality, be only mildly disconcerting. A bitter quarrel may be nothing more than a mild spat. Residents described as up in arms, just a little pissed-off. Cliché-addicted journalists make no distinctions.

A little more worrying is a phrase often used to report developments in the medical world. When you read that scientists have made a 'major breakthrough' regarding a particular life-threatening disease, the truth is probably more mundane – that they have made a small, incremental advance in their knowledge, a small step towards an eventual cure. The use of the word 'breakthrough' raises hopes – usually falsely. What, for example, happened to the following 'major breakthroughs', all enthusiastically reported in the British press in recent years? Breakthroughs ...

- ... in the search for a cure for baldness
- ... in the prevention of strokes
- ... in the search for a permanent treatment for malaria

- … in the hunt for a cure for Huntington's Disease
- … and in the battles against deafness,
- … autism,
- … obesity,
- … and diabetes?

In many cases, journalists are simply picking up on words used in a press release, the language offered by the doctors or researchers involved, who have an obvious interest in exaggerating the extent of the progress they have made.

Journalists also have a bad habit of lazily copying the precise words used by government sources – particularly in times of war. We have looked at the language of the 'degrading enemy forces' type used by politicians to minimise the horror of war. The press is often guilty of picking up and running with the same expressions.

During recent conflicts (the Falklands and two Gulf Wars) the following reporting anomalies were identified by language-watchers on both sides of the Atlantic:

- We have *armed forces* – they have a *war machine*
- We have *reporting guidelines* – they have *censorship*
- We *take out* or *suppress* – they *destroy*
- We *precision bomb* – they *fire wildly into the sky*
- Our soldiers are *professional* – their soldiers are *brainwashed*
- Our soldiers are *cautious* – their soldiers are *cowardly*
- Our soldiers are *brave* – their soldiers are *fanatical*
- Our leader is *resolute* – their leader is *defiant*
- Our leader is *statesmanlike* – their leader is *an evil dictator*

Journalists and broadcasters are also guilty of echoing the euphemisms used by terrorists to justify their actions. Ken

Bigley and other kidnap victims in Iraq were not 'executed' by their captors, as some newspapers and broadcasters reported. They were brutally murdered.

* * *

The English language contains some useful words which are frequently deployed by journalists to turn even the slightest non-story into … a story. These are the modal verbs 'could' and 'might'. See how cunningly they have been applied in these stories found during a cursory scan through one morning's papers.

> 'A new compound found in broccoli MIGHT block the effects of breast cancer, say experts.'
> But only if you eat seven kilos of the vegetable every day.

> 'Regular exercise COULD boost the immune system of OAPs to the level of 20-year-old men.'
> Or it could cause a heart attack.

> 'Venables MIGHT take over as manager of Newcastle United.'
> As, in theory, might any other football coach.

Where would modern journalists be if these and similar words were removed from their vocabulary? They MIGHT be unemployed.

Another notoriously weasely and often misleading phrase is 'linked to'. *The Times*, for example, was one of many newspapers which went to town on this story back in September 2004.

FARMED SALMON LINKED TO CANCER RISK
People who regularly eat farmed salmon may be raising
their risk of developing cancer, scientists said yesterday.

Salmon raised on British fish farms are so contaminated with carcinogenic chemicals that consumers
would be unwise to eat them more than once every
other month, a major study has concluded.

The analysis of more than 700 fish weighing more
than two tonnes in total found that farmed salmon
across Europe and North America had much higher
concentrations of 14 pollutants than fish caught from
the wild.

The chemicals, which include dioxins, DDT and
polychlorinated biphenyls (PCBs), belong to a class
known as organochlorines, which are linked to cancer
and birth defects.

Levels in the salmon bought from European
supermarkets were so high that eating more than one
portion every two months could raise a person's risk of
cancer …

This story manages to combine 'linked to', 'may be' and 'could'
in a desperate attempt to catch our attention. Eating farmed
salmon raises the risk of developing cancer by how much?
Significantly? A teensy-weensy little bit? The article doesn't
elucidate. Eating salmon may cause cancer, but then again, it
may not. The level of risk is rarely if ever established in these
stories. Perhaps it cannot be quantified. And, of course, if it
could, it would probably kill the story stone dead. 'The risk of
Scottish farmed salmon causing cancer is slightly less than the
odds against winning the national lottery jackpot in three
consecutive weeks.'

Further down the story, we learn that the research has been

carried out by scientists, not in Britain, but in America. These scientists also slip in the observation that farmed salmon in America is twice as safe as that in Britain. Scare stories are very often 'linked to' vested interest of some sort or another.

Sales of farmed salmon in Britain dipped for a week or two after this story first broke, but rapidly, and quite rightly, returned to normal levels shortly afterwards. An abnormally high incidence of cancer among regular salmon-eaters has not yet been reported. But it might.

Exciting New Book Exclusively Reveals Secrets of Our Culture of Deception

'Exclusive' is one of the most abused words in the newspaper business. It's defined in the *Concise Oxford Dictionary* as 'not published elsewhere. An article or story published by only one newspaper or periodical.' No one from any of Britain's various national newspapers seems to be aware of this definition. They seem to be working on the assumption that the word is synonymous with 'ubiquitous'.

Walking through London's Victoria Station, I noticed an *Evening Standard* poster declaring: 'Exclusive – Charles to marry Camilla.' Exclusive? I had woken that day to the radio revealing the exciting news of the impending royal marriage. The story had been trumpeted by every national and local TV and radio station all morning. Hours later, and at the same time that the *Standard* was heralding its 'exclusive', dozens of other regional evening papers were simultaneously publishing the same story.

So where is the exclusive? It must be similar to the 'Exclusive Pictures of Naked Jordan' available in almost every tabloid every day.

* * *

The deception is often in the headline.

BLAIR 'BECOMING ELECTION LIABILITY', WARN LABOUR MINISTERS

A closer inspection of this story printed in *The Observer* on 27 February 2005 reveals a slightly less dramatic story.

> Tony Blair *risks* becoming an electoral liability, according to government ministers, as the Prime Minister faces fresh accusations that his 'presidential style' is starting to affect Labour's support.

One paragraph into the story, and we are now talking only about a 'risk' of Tony Blair becoming an election liability. Let's read on.

> Officials said the Prime Minister would now adopt a less 'presidential' style, appearing in tandem with cabinet colleagues, to head off sniping about his personal unpopularity.
>
> The news follows concern that Blair's personal ratings are clouding the picture. One loyalist cabinet minister has told friends that Blair is no longer seen as an asset, particularly among traditional working-class supporters.

At last the truth emerges. Those readers who got beyond the headline and the first paragraph learn that Blair is not actually a liability, but is simply 'no longer seen as an asset'. This is journalism at its sloppiest and most misleading and we should not tolerate it in our so-called quality newspapers – or anywhere else for that matter.

There are innumerable examples of this kind of thing, but here's just one more that caught my eye. Among the stories trailed on the cover of an edition of *Word* ('the quality music magazine') was 'JULIAN CLARY: "I had a female lung transplant!"'

Turning inside, we eventually discover the less-than-dramatic truth. Julian Clary reveals: 'I remember them making fun of my voice in primary school. I concocted this theory that I'd had a lung transplant and I'd been given female lungs and that's why my voice sound like a girl's.'

Have they no shame?

Attitude, bias and market forces

Britain's national newspapers differ greatly in their tone and content. Each reflects the personal prejudices, commercial interests and political preferences of its owner and, to a much lesser extent, its editor. But they are all driven by the same irresistible market forces.

Most newspapers like to get their teeth into a good campaign. One paper might rail against the release of convicted paedophiles into the community, another against smoking in public places or, more likely, government measures to prevent it. They hope, of course, to attract readers who share their abhorrence of … whatever it is. The trouble is, the truth all too often gets lost along the way.

Since 2002, several newspapers have been loudly warning that our green and pleasant land is about to be swamped by asylum-seekers. The coverage has echoes of the Hearst/Pulitzer excesses of more than 100 years ago. *The Sun* reported that 'East European poachers' were killing and roasting swans from the Thames, while the *Daily Star* alleged that Somalians had stolen and eaten donkeys from Greenwich Park. The *Daily*

Express, amid headlines proclaiming 'Asylum Invasion' and 'Refugees, Run For Your Life', ran a story that police had arrested two Lithuanian asylum-seekers linked to Al-Qaeda who were plotting to kill the Prime Minister.

In none of these stories was any corroborative evidence available. In the case of the arrests of the two Lithuanians, police described the story as 'rubbish' and pointed out that the *Express* reporters had been told in advance that 'no security issues were raised by their arrest'.

In one 31-day period in 2003, the *Express* ran 22 front-page leads about asylum-seekers – despite protests by some of its own journalists, who considered the reports to be 'biased, distorted and racist'. In December 2004, the National Union of Journalists' general secretary, Jeremy Dear, expressed concern about the *Daily Express* 'scare stories'. He said: 'It is important if we are to propose solutions, that we understand why such inaccuracies about … asylum-seekers are published. Richard Desmond, owner of the *Express*, is said to have told one of our members working on those stories that he would keep printing them despite the criticisms because every one added 20,000 sales.'

According to one of the country's most respected journalists, 'Reporting is now so contaminated by bias and campaigning, and general mischief, that no reader can hope to get a picture of what is happening without first knowing who owns the paper, and who it is being published for.'

That was the view of former BBC political editor and editor of *The Independent*, Andrew Marr. In his book *My Trade: A Short History of British Journalism*, he says: 'The *Mirror* defines its politics as the opposite of the *Sun*'s, which in turn is defined by the geopolitics of Rupert Murdoch's News International – hostile to European federalism and the euro and so forth. If it is ferociously against Tony Blair, this is probably because Number 10 has been passing good stories to the *Sun*. Its support for Gordon Brown was, similarly, driven by the need to find a rival when Blair courted Murdoch. It felt jilted.' Marr says we need to know these things.

It's not difficult to identify a proprietor's imprimatur in our daily newspapers – not just from their political slant and general content but also from what is omitted. Scan *The Times*, *Sunday Times*, *Sun* and *News of the World*, for example, and you will find precious little reference to the monopolistic excesses of their owner Rupert Murdoch. On the other hand, you're likely to find considerable praise for the quality of films and programmes broadcast on Murdoch's Sky Television.

The reclusive and obscenely wealthy Barclay brothers recently relieved the disgraced Conrad Black of the *Daily Telegraph*, *Sunday Telegraph* and *Spectator* magazine for a price which barely put a dent in their bank balance. Sir David and Sir Frederick are comfortably placed on the list of Britain's top 50 richest people – thanks, in part, to the proceeds amassed from gambling, property and shipping businesses. But little insight into their dealings in these areas will be found in any of their newly-acquired newspapers. The business world as observed from the perspective of a *Daily Telegraph* reader is now strangely devoid of detail on the Barclay brothers' business activities. In February 2005, the *Spectator*'s media columnist, Stephen Glover, resigned after an article he had written about the plan to axe at least 90 journalists' jobs at the *Daily* and *Sunday Telegraph* was itself axed.

Journalists' work is not routinely interfered with in this way. Reporters and columnists working for national newspapers are usually fairly clear about the political, social and commercial parameters within which they are expected to operate. But the journalist who rocks the boat usually walks the gangplank.

The Times suggested that Glover's resignation made him 'a martyr to the cause of free speech'. But how many martyrs would surface at *The Times* if that nice Mr Murdoch decided to do a bit of axe-wielding?

The best of enemies

It's hardly surprising that journalists and politicians are locked together at the bottom of the list of people the public trust. To a very great extent they are dragging each other down into the gutter, relentlessly accusing each other of lying and cheating. Neither does a whole lot to enhance public faith in the other.

When Charles Clarke was Labour Party chairman, he said that the press 'have done their best to bring democratic politics into disrepute'. *The Sun* had previously expressed the view that 'too many politicians are sad, sordid, pathetic inadequate wimps with private lives that make ordinary people's stomachs churn'.

London's Mayor Ken Livingstone has accused the *Evening Standard* of waging a 'campaign of hate' against him. The paper's bosses were 'a load of scumbags and reactionary bigots', he explained.

More spleen-venting took place between politicians and the press during the 2004 Commons public administration select committee's inquiry into government communications. Editor-in-chief of the *Daily Mail*, Paul Dacre, accused Alastair Campbell, the Prime Minister's former communications chief, of being responsible for making people cynical about politics. Labour MPs on the committee retaliated by accusing Dacre's paper of 'corroding public life'.

Dacre said the government's spin machine had misrepresented the truth and manipulated the media. He cited scandals involving Bernie Ecclestone, the Hinduja brothers,

Lakshmi Mittal and Geoffrey Robinson as undermining faith in the capacity of Downing Street to tell the truth. He blamed Alastair Campbell personally for introducing a 'culture of mendacity'.

But giving evidence to the same committee, Campbell claimed that the media and not politicians were responsible for 90 per cent of what is commonly called 'spin'. He described relations between the government and the media as 'very unhealthy', and added that 'politicians are not as bad as the media who cover them'. Some journalists, he said, asked idiotic questions, wrote drivel and told lies, and if as a result he was hard on them, then 'diddums'.

Animosity between Alastair Campbell and the BBC erupted to catastrophic effect following allegations by the BBC's defence correspondent, Andrew Gilligan, that the government had 'sexed up' a Ministry of Defence report in order to justify invading Iraq. He said the government had inserted the claim that Iraq could launch weapons of mass destruction within 45 minutes, knowing it was probably wrong. Campbell repeatedly and angrily accused the corporation of bad journalism – demanding that it retract its allegation.

The story, of course, ended in the suicide of the government weapons expert Dr David Kelly after he was exposed as Gilligan's source, and in the Hutton Inquiry which cleared the government (or whitewashed it, in the view of the BBC and many other observers) of any misdeeds, Lord Hutton concluded that Gilligan's report on the Radio 4 *Today* programme was 'unfounded'. A subsequent BBC inquiry said the reporter's methods were flawed and lacked judgement.

The reality, of course, is that many journalists, both inside and outside the BBC, are guilty of far greater deviations from the truth than that committed by Andrew Gilligan. Gilligan was unfortunate that his errors of journalistic judgement, or 'honest mistakes' as he called them, got picked up by Labour's rottweiler Alastair Campbell and were used as a stick with which to beat the BBC. David Kelly became the victim of a battle between those two powerful mainstays of any free and democratic society – parliament and the press.

And those two influential institutions were again at each other's throats less than a year later when the *Daily Telegraph* accused Labour MP George Galloway of having been in the pay of Iraqi dictator Saddam Hussein. The newspaper's reporter had found documents in the Foreign Ministry in Baghdad which incriminated the politician.

The *Telegraph*'s front-page revelations emerged over several days, alleging that Galloway had received about £375,000 a year through the diversion of Iraqi 'oil for food' programme money, and that he had used a charity appeal he launched to raise money for an Iraqi girl suffering from leukaemia, as a front for personal gain. The paper implied that Galloway was guilty of treason.

The MP, who was by this time estranged from the Labour Party, immediately sued. He categorically denied all the allegations and accused the paper of thrusting a sword through his political heart. He said that the documents found in the Iraqi Foreign Ministry were crude and obvious fakes. The paper argued that it had a duty to publish such documents, even though it could not prove that they were true, and claimed its coverage had been neutral. The judge, Mr Justice Eady, said *Telegraph* executives were deluding themselves that they were covering the story neutrally: 'They did not merely adopt the allegations, they embraced them with relish and fervour. They then went on to embellish them', he said. He ordered the newspaper to pay £150,000 in damages, plus costs estimated at over £1.2 million.

On this occasion it was a victory for the honest politician

over the lying journalist – a sword through the heart of press veracity. But the war goes on.

In search of the truth

So should we believe *anything* journalists tell us?

Guardian film critic Peter Bradshaw once worked with the *Daily Mail*'s veteran columnist Peter McKay. Bradshaw says he would, from time to time, point out 'mistakes' in the great man's column. 'Laddie', McKay was wont to reply, 'you cannot expect to believe everything you write in the newspaper.'

Asked in the street if we believe what we read in the newspapers, we are, according to every MORI poll, most likely to say 'no'. But are we sure? Their influence can be subtle, working insidiously at our subconscious until, despite ourselves, we end up quoting from them in heated defence of our argument in the pub or at the dinner party. 'Well, according to an article in the *Daily Mail* you're dead wrong', we blurt out over the risotto. 'Don't believe everything you read in the newspaper' is the inevitable response.

The fact is that we do, by and large, believe what we read in the newspaper. Newspapers know their readers and know how to feed their appetites and prejudices. Author and newspaper columnist John O'Farrell suggests that if you don't believe what you read in the paper, you're probably reading the wrong one.

He offers the following advice: 'If you don't believe bogus asylum-seekers are getting grants from your local council to set up paedophile workshops – then stop reading the *Daily Mail*. If you don't believe that five-times-a-night David Beckham is having it off with another model in Barcelona – then stop reading the *Sun*. And if you don't believe that the Alpine Sprite has a wonderful tow-bar and convertible banquettes – don't read *What Caravan?*'

The only real option for the person who doesn't want to receive a distorted or partial picture of the world is to read every newspaper and try to extrapolate the truth – or, of course, to read none of them.

Journalism has a great and honourable tradition of searching for the truth. Reporters down the years have shed blood, sweat and tears, and indeed given their lives, in its pursuit. Innocent people have been freed, frauds uncovered, scandals revealed and bad politicians exposed. Journalists have been the enemy of evil and corruption wherever it raises its head.

But this, as we have seen, is only one face of journalism.

The code of conduct of the International Federation of Journalists is unequivocal on the subject of honesty: 'Respect for the truth and the rights of the public to truth is the first duty of the journalist.' Jay Rosen, Professor of Journalism and Mass Communications at New York University, concurs: 'Journalists are members of the political community, citizens themselves, and not bystanders to our public life … journalism is about recognising this truth, and trying to tell the truth at the same time.'

In his Society of Editors speech, Kevin Marsh voiced the concern that 'we don't trust those we've chosen to exercise power for us; and we don't trust those who tell us how the chosen are doing it. And that', he concluded, 'cannot be good.'

Amen.

CHAPTER EIGHT

Dirty rotten lies

Scotsman Arthur Ferguson seemed like an honest person. A succession of American visitors to London in the 1920s never doubted that he owned the properties he was offering to sell them.

They were sufficiently beguiled by his elaborate lies to hand over considerable amounts of money. A £1,000 down payment, for example, bought them Big Ben. For £2,000 down they received the keys to Buckingham Palace and for a one-off payment of £6,000 they got the whole of Trafalgar Square. Nelson's Column and the Houses of Parliament were among his other irresistible offers.

In 1925 Ferguson moved his scam to America, where he sold the White House to a rancher who handed over $100,000 as a first instalment. His deception eventually unravelled when he tried to sell the Statue of Liberty to a visiting Australian, who went to the police.

Not to be outdone, rival conman 'Count' Victor Lustig succeeded in selling the Eiffel Tower to two separate scrap metal merchants before the gendarmes finally caught up with him.

Both Ferguson and Lustig were talented but unprincipled liars. Their deceptions earned them a great deal of money – though both were eventually caught and sent to prison. They were not amateur liars like you and me. They were professionals, for whom lies and deception were basic tools of the trade. They had taken the talent we all demonstrate from a very young age, and honed it to selfish and criminal purpose.

The world is not short of people who will take advantage of the gullibility or greed of others to extort and cheat. The confidence trickster is just one of the species of black-hearted but silver-tongued villains who occupy the darkest and dankest undergrowth of the jungle of lies in which we live. And there's nothing new about this manipulative crime.

In 1644 the self-styled Witch-Finder General, Matthew Hopkins, began his quest to rid English villages of their witches. It was, in effect, a deadly confidence trick, and it made Hopkins a great deal of money. He could earn as much as £20 per village – a fortune in those days. But his claimed ability to identify witches was pure invention. Witches were believed not to bleed, so he would use a knife with a retractable blade to pretend to pierce the flesh of an accused woman. Hopkins then applied sleep deprivation – keeping his victims awake for up to three days in order to extract a confession. During a two-year career, he had more than 100 people executed for witchcraft, before suspicions about his tactics grew and he was eventually forced out of business.

Some 80 years later, Mary Tofts gained fame and some fortune by convincing not only the public, but also George I, that she had given birth to a number of rabbits. Nathaniel St Andre, surgeon-anatomist to the King, examined 'the Godalming rabbit-breeder' and reported back that he had witnessed the delivery of two stillborn rabbits 'or portions thereof'. The King, apparently, was impressed.

Mary went on to produce a total of sixteen rabbits – all, sadly, stillborn. Though described as being of 'very stupid and sullen temper', she'd managed to achieve the deception by the simple technique of 'pushing the rabbits up inside her'. Eventually, when suspicious authorities threatened an operation to examine the phenomenon, she confessed her hoax. A woman had put her up to it, apparently, and had provided the rabbits. And off Mary hopped to Bridewell prison.

The best-known of modern conmen is probably Frank Abagnale, portrayed by Leonardo DiCaprio in the Spielberg biopic *Catch Me If You Can*. In the mid-1960s, the teenager posed as an airline pilot, a doctor and a lawyer, cashing fake cheques to the value of more than $2 million. Abagnale was eventually caught and imprisoned. He served five years before emerging a reformed character, to become one of the world's most respected experts on identity and cheque fraud. Many corporations and law enforcement agencies have adopted his fraud prevention programmes. Abagnale said: 'I consider my past immoral, unethical and illegal. It is something I am not proud of.'

The image of conmen as amiable rogues, like the characters portrayed by Paul Newman and Robert Redford in *The Sting*, whose victims or 'marks' were greedy villains who got exactly what they deserved, is almost entirely false. Conmen more commonly persuade the elderly to hand over their pension money for 'safe-keeping', or encourage people to invest their life savings in non-existent companies. They are guilty of mean crimes which can destroy people's lives.

They are people like 34-year-old Robert Hendy-Freegard, described by DS Bob Brandon of the Metropolitan Police as the most accomplished liar he had ever encountered in 25 years in the force. The former barman, posing as a spy, tricked his eight victims out of almost £1 million before he was caught. Found guilty of multiple offences of kidnapping, theft and deception, he was jailed for life in September 2005. The court heard how he told his victims that they were being hunted by the IRA and that their lives were in danger. They were physically abused and psychologically traumatised. Some, the jury was told, would never fully recover from the experience.

* * *

We saw in Chapter 2 that brain scans have shown that our basic, primary instinct is to tell the truth, but that we have an equally natural, secondary facility to resist that instinct – to tell lies. In other words, we have a choice. Criminal liars liberally exercise that secondary facility. Their crimes take advantage of their victims' gullibility and greed, but also exploit a more noble human impulse – to trust.

Our society is built on a broad foundation of trust. Though most of us can whip up a fair bit of cynicism when it suits us, most of the time we choose to believe what our parents, friends, colleagues and even politicians tell us. And this despite considerable evidence that they are actually lying a lot of the time.

We believe most of what we are told, both because we need to and because we want to. We want to believe our parents when they tell us there is a Santa Claus. We want to believe our friends when they compliment our limited cooking skills. Neville Chamberlain wanted to believe Hitler when he told him he had no further military ambitions.

And we need to believe that people are telling the truth because the alternative is unthinkable. What kind of dysfunctional world would it be if we always thought people were lying, if we were always suspicious, took nothing on face value, questioned everyone's motives, double-checked everything we were told, never accepted a compliment, always assumed that a promise would be broken and all commitments would be reneged upon – and no longer believed there was a Father Christmas?

Without trust we would no longer co-operate with each other, and society would collapse. Though, as we'll explore in the final chapter, things might be just as bad in a world in which no one lied.

A world-wide web of deception

Mass communication has now opened up opportunities for a new and insidious 'crime of persuasion'. The icy fingers of duplicity can now reach out into all of our homes – taking advantage of our trusting natures.

You've got mail:

Hello,

I am the wife of international best-selling author Brian King who is currently incarcerated in a British jail, falsely accused of plagiarism.

Before his arrest Brian managed to deposit 5 million copies of his latest book, *The Lying Ape*, in a bank vault in Potters Bar. He would be willing to transfer 20 per cent of the books to a lock-up garage near you, if you would just send £5,000 to enable him to bribe his guards to unlock his manacles for ten minutes so he can scratch his nose and arrange to transfer the copies of his book (a rattling good read, says *Lying Apes Weekly*) to your garage.

Please help my husband. He is completely innocent.

Yours sincerely
Mrs King

Convincing? Well, possibly not. The prospect of more than

5 million copies of this book being printed is, sadly, somewhat remote. But propositions not much more plausible than this arrive by email, fax and post to homes and businesses around the world on a frighteningly regular basis.

For those of you not familiar with the modus operandi, here's a real example:

DEAR SIR:
I HAVE BEEN REQUESTED BY THE NIGERIAN NATIONAL PETROLEUM COMPANY TO CONTACT YOU FOR ASSISTANCE IN RESOLVING A MATTER. THE NIGERIAN NATIONAL PETROLEUM COMPANY HAS RECENTLY CONCLUDED A LARGE NUMBER OF CONTRACTS FOR OIL EXPLORATION IN THE SUB-SAHARA REGION. THE CONTRACTS HAVE IMMEDIATELY PRODUCED MONEYS EQUALLING US$40,000,000. THE NIGERIAN NATIONAL PETROLEUM COMPANY IS DESIROUS OF OIL EXPLORATION IN OTHER PARTS OF THE WORLD, HOWEVER, BECAUSE OF CERTAIN REGULATIONS OF THE NIGERIAN GOVERNMENT, IT IS UNABLE TO MOVE THESE FUNDS TO ANOTHER REGION.

YOUR ASSISTANCE IS REQUESTED AS A NON-NIGERIAN CITIZEN TO ASSIST THE NIGERIAN NATIONAL PETROLEUM COMPANY, AND ALSO THE CENTRAL BANK OF NIGERIA, IN MOVING THESE FUNDS OUT OF NIGERIA. IF THE FUNDS CAN BE TRANSFERRED TO YOUR NAME, IN YOUR ACCOUNT, THEN YOU CAN FORWARD THE FUNDS AS DIRECTED BY THE NIGERIAN NATIONAL PETROLEUM COMPANY.

IN EXCHANGE FOR YOUR ACCOMMODATING
SERVICES, THE NIGERIAN NATIONAL PETRO-
LEUM COMPANY WOULD AGREE TO ALLOW
YOU TO RETAIN 10%, OR US$4 MILLION OF
THIS AMOUNT.

HOWEVER, TO BE A LEGITIMATE TRANSFEREE
OF THESE MONEYS ACCORDING TO NIGERIAN
LAW, YOU MUST PRESENTLY BE A DEPOSITOR
OF AT LEAST US$100,000 IN A NIGERIAN BANK
WHICH IS REGULATED BY THE CENTRAL BANK
OF NIGERIA.

PLEASE CALL ME AT YOUR EARLIEST CON-
VENIENCE AT 18-467-4975. TIME IS OF THE
ESSENCE IN THIS MATTER; VERY QUICKLY THE
NIGERIAN GOVERNMENT WILL REALIZE THAT
THE CENTRAL BANK IS MAINTAINING THIS
AMOUNT ON DEPOSIT, AND ATTEMPT TO LEVY
CERTAIN DEPOSITORY TAXES ON IT.

FROM: DR ALTAKA YURMANI
CENTRAL BANK OF NIGERIA
LAGOS, NIGERIA

There are a great many variations on this theme, many of them
emanating from Nigeria and most of them, for no obvious
reason, WRITTEN IN CAPITAL LETTERS. The name of the
correspondent may change, but the central message remains
constant: 'Send us some money and we will make you rich
beyond your wildest dreams.'

But nobody would be deceived by these transparent lies,
would they? It seems they would – like flies caught in a world-
wide web of deception. Losses from 'Nigerian Advanced Fee

Fraud Email Scams' are put at over $1 million every day in the US alone. In Britain the average victim is conned out of more than £50,000. The National Criminal Intelligence Service estimates that £150 million is lost to the UK economy every year.

The people behind these scams are demonstrating astonishing confidence in their ability to deceive. Interpol has evidence that some fraudsters are contacting previous victims, posing as Nigerian government officials investigating the fraud, requesting an up-front payment before their money is recovered.

Inspiration for this crime, by the way, may well have been a poor farm boy called Oscar Hartzell, who, during the American Depression, dreamed up the idea of contacting everybody in the Midwest whose surname was Drake, and telling them that they stood to benefit from the unclaimed fortune left by the English seaman Sir Francis Drake. With interest it amounted to $100 billion. All they had to do was contribute to the costs of taking the British government to court to retrieve the money. He promised a $500 return for every dollar invested. The cash poured in from all over America, from rich and poor alike. Church ministers sent donations from their congregations. Even after his scam was rumbled, people kept sending Hartzell money – in prison.

Modern internet advanced fee fraud is just one manifestation of a virus of online deceptions. A computer fool can also be separated from his or her money via bogus online auctions, fake advanced fee loan schemes and phony business investment opportunities.

In May 2005, a survey by internet service provider AOL revealed that one in twenty UK internet users had lost money through online scams. Almost half of them had received so-called phishing e-mails aimed at tricking them into revealing details such as online banking passwords.

Cyberspace is littered with liars.

Denial

Very few criminals respond to being arrested by saying 'It's a fair cop. I'll go quietly.' The instinct to deny guilt is developed at a tender age. As we saw earlier, when young children were left in a room and told not to look at a toy placed behind them, almost all turned to look at it. When questioned afterwards, all but a handful of the three- and four-year-olds refused to admit that they had peeked.

Adults demonstrate precisely the same behaviour, particularly when accused of a crime. 'I couldn't have done it. I was in Margate.' 'I got those grazes on my knuckles from playing conkers.' 'I've never seen that crowbar / stolen credit card / sawn-off shotgun / bag of cocaine before in my life.'

Ever since I first tried to get a US visa I have wondered if any one has ever succumbed to the application form's invitation to admit that they are guilty of any of an extraordinary range of crimes.

Applicants are told to tick 'yes' or 'no' to such questions as:

- Have you ever unlawfully distributed or sold a controlled substance (drug), or been a prostitute or procurer for prostitutes?
- Do you seek to enter the United States to engage in export control violations, subversive or terrorist activities, or any other unlawful purpose? Are you a member or representative of a terrorist organisation as currently designated by the US Secretary of State? Have you ever participated in persecutions directed by the Nazi government of Germany; or have you ever participated in genocide?

In order to encourage drug dealers, prostitutes, terrorists, Nazis and genocidal maniacs to fill in the form honestly, the US State Department thoughtfully adds:

- A YES answer does not automatically signify ineligibility for a visa.

Meanwhile in Britain, confessing to murder still automatically gets you into trouble with the law. In December 1996, former model Tracie Andrews took denial to an extraordinary length, inventing an elaborate sequence of lies to disguise the fact that she had murdered her boyfriend, Lee Harvey, by stabbing him 30 times in the chest. She told police that Lee had been the victim of a 'road rage' attack. The driver of another vehicle, 'a fat man with staring eyes', had chased their car for more than five miles, then dragged her boyfriend from their vehicle and stabbed him to death.

Tracie Andrews' lies were exposed in court and she was jailed for life. Ironically, a false denial can sometimes be more convincing than an honest one. Professional, criminal liars are, to a large extent, prepared to be confronted; they have their story neatly worked out and can usually deliver it with conviction. The innocent person falsely accused of a crime often appears to be lying when trying to plead innocence in the face of damning circumstantial evidence.

Australian Lindy Chamberlain served more than three years of a life sentence with hard labour for the murder of her baby daughter Azaria, before evidence eventually emerged supporting her claim that a dingo had snatched the child from their tent while the family were camping near Ayers Rock. Her original testimony in court was considered to be rather cold and emotionless and had led the jury to assume her guilt.

More recently, a succession of British women who also failed to convince juries that they had not murdered their infant children have been released from prison after the evidence on which they were convicted was discredited.

Donna Anthony from Yeovil was jailed for life in 1998 for

killing her eleven-month-old daughter Jordan and four-month-old son Michael. She was released in April 2005 after an Appeal Court judge said evidence given at her trial by paediatrician Professor Sir Roy Meadow had been 'significantly undermined'.

Professor Meadow had also given evidence in the cases of Sally Clarke and Angela Canning, each also accused of double infanticide. Meadow said the chances of two siblings dying of 'cot death syndrome' were one in 73 million. For members of a jury, trying to establish truth from lies, the evidence of an eminent scientist like Professor Meadow weighed heavily against protestations of innocence by grieving mothers. The juries believed the professor and not the mothers – but they were wrong.

Professor Meadow had made a fundamental mathematical error. Appeal courts were told that the odds of two siblings suffering cot deaths were in fact only around one in 100. Sally Clarke and Angela Canning were both released from prison, their convictions quashed. They had been telling the truth. In 2004, the Attorney General announced a review of another 297 similar cases.

Miscarriages of justice are not uncommon. The legal system cannot always distinguish the liar from the honest person. Nobody can know, of course, how many innocent people are currently languishing in jail, any more than they can know how many guilty liars have poked justice in the eye.

* * *

False allegations of child abuse can be an occupational hazard for care workers, teachers and other people who work professionally with young people. Lawyer Michael Ive specialises in acting for clients who he believes have been wrongfully accused of child abuse. He argues that the police and court system has developed an unhealthy assumption that if a child makes an allegation against an adult, they must be telling the truth.

During the past four years Ive has represented about 50 men who claimed to have been falsely accused of sexually abusing children. The cases all went to trial and all but two of his clients were found not guilty. How could so many innocent people have found themselves in this situation? Ive says:

> The problem is that children's allegations about abuse are not investigated properly by the police. They assume the child is not lying and it is therefore up to the adult involved to prove he is innocent. There are child protection officers in every police station and they all seem to have been brought up in the belief that children do not lie. It's a type of tunnel vision.

Psychologists' studies revealing the capacity of young children to lie come as no surprise to Ive. He says: 'In my experience, children can be amazingly manipulative. It's unbelievable. They will tell any lie. My clients are put in the difficult position of having to prove that the child is lying.'

He says it's particularly difficult to challenge a child's lies within the courtroom environment. 'You are always treading on egg shells. If you challenge a child's testimony and he or she bursts into tears, the jury automatically sympathises with the child, to the detriment of the defendant's case.'

Michael Ive's approach is to investigate the background of the complaint.

> Unlike the police, we leave no stone unturned. We look at school reports, social services records, earlier complaints and previous applications for compensation for sexual abuse. We try to find a motive for the accusation.

The motive might be that Mum and Dad have separated. The child lives with Dad who won't let the child see Mum, perhaps for good reason. The child might then suggest that Dad is 'doing stuff to me'. Or the motive might be financial. The child's parents will encourage him or her to claim they have been molested in order to claim compensation.

Lies, whether about murder, sexual abuse or taking a chocolate biscuit, are intractable things. Once we commit ourselves to a lie, as a child or an adult, it tends to stay told – the consequences of coming clean becoming greater the longer we hold out. Lies don't mellow with age; they grow roots and become cancerous. The truth doesn't really stand a chance.

The theatre of lies

Anyone entering a criminal court hoping to hear 'the truth, the whole truth and nothing but the truth' is likely to leave disappointed. Though its function is to accommodate a collective search for the truth, the law court is, more often than not, a theatre of lies. The British justice system is based on accusation and refutation. Allowing for the fact that some defendants are actually innocent and their accusers honestly mistaken, in all other cases lying is an innate part of the process. Either the accuser is lying, or the defendant is.

That a guilty defendant might lie to save his skin isn't surprising. But who else is guilty of deception in the courtroom scenario? Surely not the lawyers. Lawyers are solid, upright citizens, pillars of society, foot soldiers in the war against injustice and evil. They sign our passport application forms. We trust them. Yes, we know they can confuse us with their 'hereinafters' and 'parties of the first part' and other legalese nonsense, but they wouldn't actually lie, would they?

In Thomas More's *Utopia* the populace 'have no lawyers among them, for they consider them, as a sort of people whose profession is to disguise matters'. Jonathan Swift described lawyers as 'a society of men … bred up from their youth in the art of proving by words multiplied for the purpose that white is black, and black is white, according as they are paid.'

Modern observers are a little more circumspect. Social scientist J.A. Barnes writes that 'lawyers can twist and distort the grammatical form of the questions they put to witnesses according to the kind of response they are seeking to elicit.' He adds: 'It would, I suppose, be stretching the concept of deceit unduly to say that asking the legendary question "when did you stop beating your wife?" is an attempt to deceive, but it's certainly an attempt to trap.'

Professional rules require lawyers, in most circumstances, to refuse to defend a client they *know* to be guilty. But if a lawyer only *suspects* that a client is lying, he is expected to use every argument and tactic available to him to achieve an acquittal, if necessary by exploiting loopholes in the law or technical irregularities in the process of bringing the charges.

Solicitor Paul Drew has successfully defended many clients in circumstances where he has had, at least, serious suspicions that they might be guilty. What would he say if a client came to him with an entirely preposterous assertion of innocence?

I would say that I believe him – because he is my client – but that a jury wouldn't, and that if the client continues to defend the case and is found guilty he will not be given credit for an early guilty plea. If he insists on going ahead it makes you think that maybe he is telling the truth after all.

Drew recalled one client, a mother of four children, who had been arrested by the police for possession of drugs with intent to supply. She claimed that the police had planted the drugs on her. Despite severe reservations about her story, he went ahead and defended her in court. The jury, however, were not convinced and she received a suspended prison sentence. At his client's insistence, he then initiated a civil claim for damages against the police. The police eventually settled after the two officers involved refused to give evidence. Paul Drew was left wondering who, after all, had been lying.

A lawyer's responsibility to do his utmost for his client can lead to some ridiculous defence arguments, as in a case which came before a Los Angeles court back in July 1992.

Alleged arsonist Douglas Hunziker, according to his attorney, was the victim of an extraordinary series of coincidences. Witnesses at his arson trial had said the 22-year-old former firefighter trainee was present at nine of the ten blazes he was charged with setting, often helping to put out the flames or to evacuate people from the area.

The strange sequence of events began during Fourth of July festivities, when Hunziker called firefighters to a blaze in a trash container in front of his home. During the following few weeks Hunziker was closely associated with another nine fires, including a blaze at a four-car garage at the home of his ex-girlfriend just days after the couple had broken up, and another at the Comedy and Magic Club where Hunziker was working. Two days later a second fire at the club forced the evacuation of more than 200 people. And shortly after that a blaze broke out at a local driving school which the defendant attended.

But just because Hunziker was at nine fires in less than seven months didn't mean he started them, said his defence attorney Darryl Genis. 'It is entirely plausible', he told the jury, 'that Douglas Hunziker is nothing more than a victim of extremely bad luck.'

No jury in any land was going to swallow that particular defence, but Paul Drew concedes that clearly some guilty defendants, aided by an able lawyer, will get away with their crime, even, literally, with murder. 'The defendant is innocent until proven guilty and the prosecution is required to prove its case', he says. 'These principles are essential to the British legal system. It does mean that some guilty people will get away with their lies, but there is more at stake than just the truth. The rule of law and criminal procedures, which are essential to justice, are also important – as important as the truth.'

Once the guilty defendant has told his first big courtroom lie – 'not guilty, your honour' – a whole panoply of supporting lies naturally follows. These are then aided and abetted by the defence lawyer, who only *thinks* they are a load of codswallop; he doesn't *know* it.

Others engaged in the theatre of lies are the witnesses, both for the defence and the prosecution. Any number of motives can account for their lack of truthfulness. They may be friends, family or criminal accomplices of the defendant. Or they may be prosecution witnesses, including police, who have their own motives for wanting to see 'justice done' whatever it takes.

Canadian psychologist Dr Tana Dineen worries that courts in North America are developing an unhealthy tolerance for lies.

'Lying under oath is just something everybody does', she says. The police apparently have taken to calling it 'testilying'. The O.J. Simpson trial, says Dineen, provided many examples of police perjuring themselves at the witness stand. The trial judge remarked that two officers in particular had demonstrated a 'reckless disregard for the truth'. But he took no action against them. 'We live in an era when even the most flagrant disregard for the truth brings little more than harsh words from judges', says Dineen.

She quotes Judge Roderic Duncan of the Alamada County Superior Court in California as saying that lying under oath had become an accepted element in most trials. The Judge had described an occasion when he reported a 'slamdunk case of perjury' to the local prosecutor, pointing out that the witness had 'admitted in my court that he had lied under oath'. Again, no action was taken.

Dineen concludes:

> When our courts tolerate even the blackest of lies, we risk losing not only any sense that their verdicts are based on truth, but our faith in the moral principle of truth itself. If our courts show a disregard for veracity, then how is it possible for us to assume that anyone really cares about truth-telling? If we can't trust our courts to uphold the principle of truth-telling, then who can we trust?

I rest my case.

CHAPTER NINE

Pants on fire

The world, we must by now agree, is full of liars who are hell bent (as well as hell bound, apparently) on misleading and deceiving us – and determined to rob us blind. It would therefore be handy if we could easily identify them, if they had distinguishing characteristics which marked them out in a crowd.

If their pants were on fire, or their hair stuck up like a telephone wire, we could take appropriate avoiding action, refusing to believe a single word they say. But the pants of the liar do not, alas, spontaneously combust, and their hair can easily be plastered flat with gel. So can noses give the game away?

'Where are the gold pieces now?' the Fairy asked.
'I lost them', answered Pinocchio, but he told a lie, for he had them in his pocket.
As he spoke, his nose, long though it was, became at least two inches longer.
'And where did you lose them?'
'In the wood nearby.'
At this second lie, his nose grew a few more inches …

Research exclusively undertaken for this book reveals that the average nose dimensions of estate agents, politicians and second-hand car salesmen are precisely in line with the national average. Thus fails the Pinocchio Solution.

Liars resolutely refuse to wear T-shirts declaring 'Dirty Rotten Liar', but they do have a habit of revealing themselves, like the inveterate thief who claims to be living on the dole but who throws money around like there's no tomorrow, or the office manager who takes the credit for a junior colleague's initiative but comes unstuck when his own superior quizzes him for details. And of course there's the adulterous husband who returns home from his 'night out with the boys' with lipstick on his collar.

But these are not good liars. They are bad, clumsy, inadequate liars. Good liars are much harder to spot. They are, at one extreme, people like Harold Shipman, the worst serial killer in British history, an entirely harmless-looking family practitioner. For decades, while reassuring patients that he was acting in their best interests, Shipman was secretly murdering them. Here was a polished liar with no evil laugh or sinister staring eye – no wonder he proved so hard to catch. The Yorkshire Ripper, Peter Sutcliffe, was brought in for questioning on no fewer than nine occasions by detectives investigating his horrific murders. Time after time he was released, having convinced his inquisitors that he was innocent. Sutcliffe, like Shipman, was an excellent liar.

Short of applying electric shocks or ripping out fingernails, how can the truth be extracted from the determined dissembler or bland emotionless liar? The old Good Cop / Bad Cop technique, an effective but never entirely legitimate way of identifying criminal lies, was scuppered by the Police and Criminal Evidence Act 1984 which required interviews to be recorded.

But there is good news. Psychologists, psychiatrists and electronics engineers are determinedly on the case and hope soon to have the liars on the run. And we're not just talking about mass-murderers. Techniques and technology already exist to help us detect even the most modest of dissembling.

The secret of detecting lies goes far beyond identifying the basic implausibility of a statement, or the superficial body movements that accompany the words. These signals, as we will see, can themselves be deceptive. Many people develop the habit of embellishing their accounts of events in their lives with entertaining but fictional detail. It makes the story better. But the most outrageous and least plausible elements can often turn out to be true. It's very easy to draw the wrong conclusion. Fact, as we know, is very often stranger than fiction. If your employee's absence really was the result of his being abducted by aliens, or the lipstick on your husband's collar was genuinely deposited by an attractive stranger who had mistaken him for Tom Cruise, you're going to take some convincing. The fact that your employee/husband appears to be embarrassed by his story reinforces your conviction that he's lying – even if he isn't. To accurately detect the true liar, we must go deeper.

The obvious place to start is with the words themselves. In his book *Detecting Lies and Deceit*, psychologist Aldert Vrij explains the complex techniques which can be applied to measure whether or not a verbal statement is true. A method known as Statement Validity Assessment, developed in Germany originally to determine the credibility of child witnesses, is accepted as evidence in courts in a number of European countries, though not in the UK. It involves:

- A structured interview
- A 'criteria-based content analysis' that systematically assesses the content and quality of the statement

- Evaluation of the outcome via a set of questions known as a Validity Check-list.

Statement Validity Assessment is designed principally to confirm that someone is telling the truth – not to detect lies. To identify lies, Vrij argues, we need to dig deeper. We need to apply 'Reality Monitoring'. This acknowledges that memories of real experience differ from memories based on fiction and that people actually speak differently when recalling them. Reality monitoring can, in theory, spot the false account.

And it's not just what we say, it's the way we say it. Aldert Vrij looks for indicators of deceit within tone of voice, pitch, speed and volume of speech and the length of pauses. He also concludes that liars make more implausible answers, give shorter responses, make fewer self-references and give more indirect replies.

But it's not that simple, of course. Most psychologists agree that no amount of speech analysis can be really effective unless it's weighed in with other clues to our emotions.

An expert lie-spotter, like American psychologist Paul Ekman, can detect a falsehood from a subtle mixture of signals including language, body posture and facial micro-expressions. He says people would lie less if they thought there was one single sign of lying – but there isn't. There is no sign of deceit itself – no gesture, expression or muscle twitch that means a person is lying. There are only clues that the person is poorly prepared, and clues of emotions that don't fit what the person is saying.

'It is not a simple matter to catch lies', says Paul Ekman. 'One problem is the barrage of information. There is too much to consider at once. Too many sources – words, pauses, sound of the voice, expressions, head movements, gestures, posture, respiration, flushing or blanching, sweating and so on. And all of these sources may transmit information simultaneously or in overlapping time, competing for the lie-catcher's attention.'

Ekman thinks that 'micro-expressions' provide the best clues to whether or not someone is lying.

> One is looking for discrepancies – where the face is telling you something different to the words. If I say to you 'I don't mind your criticism, it was very useful' and at the same time my lips are narrowing, a sign of anger, there is a discrepancy. I am trying to conceal my anger. These are subtle but reliable signs that most people miss. If I say 'that was a wonderful thing you did' and smile broadly, but the skin between my eyebrows doesn't come down a bit – it is not a true smile, just a social smile, which suggests I don't mean what I say.

And it's very hard, if not impossible, to fake these micro-expressions. 'We can fabricate signs of emotion', says Ekman, 'but we will not be employing certain key facial muscles which are very hard to control.' Asymmetry is another clue to deceit. Crooked expressions, in which the actions are slightly stronger on one side of the face than the other, are an indication that the feeling shown is not felt.

TV magician and illusionist Derren Brown has built a successful career on his understanding of human behaviour, often using subtle verbal and visual suggestions to influence and manipulate what people think and do. His skill at recognising the difference between the way people behave when they are lying or telling the truth is also demonstrated in his act.

He will, for example, invite passers-by in the street to present him with a number of pieces of information, some of which are true, some false. He identifies the lies with uncanny accuracy. On one occasion he asked a second-hand car salesperson to silently think of five things she could claim about a car on the forecourt, four of which were true and one false. Watching her face intently as she considered each claim in turn, Brown correctly identified, from her expressions alone, the false thought.

Together with writer and broadcaster Martin Plimmer, I visited Brown to put his skills to the test. Under my watchful gaze, he asked Martin a few general questions and then invited him to think of his first pet, and then to offer him five different names, only one of which was true. Martin slowly and precisely intoned: 'Baby, Billy, Booby, Bob and Beauty.' Brown spotted that Martin changed from an upward to a downward inflection after his third suggestion, which indicated that he was no longer looking for a response. Brown therefore deduced that Martin's first pet (a cat incidentally) was called Booby. He was correct.

Further tell-tale signs can be found in the eyes, he explained:

My approach is to look for the truth pattern and look for how it is broken. So, for example, if I ask what you had for dinner last night, as you think about it, your natural response will be for your eyes to move somewhere; more often than not it is up and to the left if you are trying to remember something. Your eye movement correlates to the part of the brain you are using.

But if I ask what you want for breakfast tomorrow, or how would you like to decorate your house – where the thing hasn't happened and you have to construct information – you have to use a different part of the brain and your eyes will, correspondingly, move to a different place.

So Brown watches how someone's eyes move when they are telling (or even thinking) the truth, so that he can recognise a lie when the pattern of eye movement changes.

> Some people say eyes moving to the left means you are remembering an image, eyes to the right means you are constructing an image. That's rubbish. People's eyes will go somewhere, and it will happen reliably if they are remembering information and they will break that pattern if they are talking about the future or telling a lie.

As he got up to leave, I asked him if we should believe everything we see in his stage act. He was, of course, accused of cheating in his infamous 'Russian roulette' routine – of using blanks instead of live bullets. 'Everything I say in my act is God's honest truth', he said.

I'd like to believe him.

* * *

So it seems that pretty much everything we say and do betrays our lies and deceit. All we need is the ability to recognise the signs, an ability which most of us, unfortunately, don't have.

At the University of Central Lancashire, psychologist Paul Seagar puts our lie-spotting abilities to the test. In clinical experiments, he runs videos of people being interviewed and asks participants to say whether they think they are lying or telling the truth, and to indicate their level of confidence in the choice.

Seagar's first conclusion is that people who believe they are intuitive tend to be among the worst at spotting lies. Police officers, whose job requires them to evaluate the honesty of people, fared no better in these tests than any other group. Their accuracy rate ranged from 45 per cent to 60 per cent, averaging out at 50 per cent. No better than flipping a coin. Interestingly, people tend to be better at spotting truth than lies. This, it transpires, is because we have a 'truth bias' and want to believe that people are honest. The test participants identified people telling the truth about 70 per cent of the time, but they spotted the liars in only 35 per cent of cases.

A similar study at the University of San Francisco reported that around 1 in 400 people seem to have particular talent for spotting lies, but, as in Britain, none of these gifted few were police officers.

Seagar admits that he expected the police to achieve better than average results, but was proved wrong. What distinguished the police officers tested was that they all demonstrated a high level of confidence in their judgement. Other psychological studies have drawn the conclusion that many professional lie-catchers, like police or immigration officers, misread or over-estimate the significance of people's body language as an indicator of lying. They fail to understand that only a complex analysis of the combination of body language, speech and micro-expressions will reveal the full story.

'People build up stereotypes', says Seagar:

They think liars move around nervously and avoid eye-contact, but this is generally incorrect. Research shows that because lying is cognitively difficult, people have to concentrate on what they are about to say, and hardly shift about at all. All of their attention is focused on what they are about to say. Also, the clever, practised liar knows that people expect liars to be agitated, so they will make a particular effort to sit still and hold eye contact.

On my baby's eyes

Hendon Police College Instructor Steve Savell spent many years on the beat, being lied to on a regular basis. Despite what the psychologists say, Savell remains confident about his ability to spot the criminal liar. 'When you stop someone who has something to hide, they immediately start acting', he says. 'It's instantly recognisable. You can see a pattern of behaviour. You then have to trip them up with clever questioning.'

For example, if he suspected someone had given him a false name and address, Savell would simply ask for details, including postcode, go on to ask about the suspect's date of birth, even star sign, and then suddenly ask for the postcode again. 'If they suddenly have to stop and think, it is not the same behaviour. It is easy for a copper on the street to spot these nuances,' he says.

Once his suspicion was aroused, Savell would then 'put it to the suspect' that he or she was guilty of the crime in question. 'In my experience, guilty people will often come out with the same reaction. They say "on my baby's eyes, it wasn't me". As soon as they say that you know they are lying.'

It's an interesting theory, though not one that Paul Seagar would accept as entirely foolproof. He wants to raise the standard of lie-detection by police, customs officers and others to around 80 per cent accuracy. 'We would put them through tests which would show them that they are not as good as they think they are', he says. 'It will dispel their assumptions about how people act and react when lying or telling the truth, and we can then start to train them to become better lie-detectors.'

But PC Savell thinks that many felons are capable of keeping ahead of the game. 'If a criminal is good at what he does, he will learn the systems of detecting lies and work out a way to beat it. I prefer good old-fashioned policing methods – and evidence. Evidence is excellent.'

It would seem that it takes a liar to know a liar. Back in the 1990s, tests of lie-detecting skills were carried out on prison officers and their inmates. The inmates won hands down.

* * *

John Freeman, who runs the Special Investigation Unit of loss adjusters CAPITA MacLarens, is confident in his ability to spot insurance fraud liars. 'Surveys reveal that 23 per cent of people know or have known someone who has exaggerated an insurance claim', he says. 'Twenty-two per cent think it does no harm and 16 per cent think you won't get caught. But I'm here to tell you they do.'

Freeman doesn't think there are any really good liars. He believes they all trip themselves up as soon as questioning gets detailed:

> People start with small lies, but then have to build on them as we ask more questions. Where did you buy the Rolex watch you claim to have lost? What were you doing when you lost it? We keep probing and eventually find they haven't thought it all through and cannot maintain the lie. They then usually offer to withdraw their claim. It is up to the insurance company whether or not to prosecute in such cases.

Rolex watches are the items most commonly listed in fraudulent insurance claims. Freeman believes that if everyone who claimed to have lost their Rolex on a beach had actually done so, the seashore would be knee-deep in the ostentatious timepieces.

Some lies are easily spotted. One householder claimed for a carpet which had been ruined by having paint spilled on it. Several months after the claim was submitted, Freeman phoned the claimant and arranged a visit to the house. When he arrived, the paint on the carpet was still wet.

Other fraudulent claims require extensive and detailed questioning before the truth emerges. A businessman who had, in reality, set fire to his factory claimed that he had been on holiday when the premises burned down. As soon as Freeman started to ask him who he had booked the holiday through, the name of the hotel and what the weather had been like, the whole fiction unravelled and the truth emerged. The man went to jail.

The Association of British Insurers says that people making fraudulent claims on their household and car insurance policies alone costs the industry £20 million a week. That's a lot of money – and a lot of lies.

Technology

If the average person can detect lies only 35 per cent of the time, even when focused on the task in experimental conditions, it follows that we are extremely unlikely to spot them in our normal, unguarded life. Most liars, it seems, can fool most people most of the time.

John Freeman and other insurance fraud investigators do have some technology at their disposal. Voice stress analysers plugged into phone lines identify signs of anxiety in callers, and 'video spectral comparators' and 'electric static document analysers' help to pinpoint when documents such as receipts have been tampered with. Otherwise, they must rely on shrewd questioning and intuition.

What's needed is a foolproof machine; some sort of technology which takes the hard work out of spotting deception – a box of tricks which will ring an alarm bell if it hears a lie.

The polygraph test has been around for a long time. Though viewed with suspicion in Britain, its use in the United States is widespread and growing. More than a million tests are administered every year. It's most commonly used by private employers, including McDonald's, to check out prospective employees. Some, but not all, states allow its results to be submitted as evidence in court if both defence and prosecution agree. Defence attorneys will go down this path if the prosecution agree to drop the case if the polygraph shows that the suspect is telling the truth.

It's completely inaccurate to refer to a polygraph as a lie-detector. It does not and cannot detect lies. The machine measures the 'autonomic nervous system signs of arousal' – breathing rate, pulse, blood pressure and perspiration – physiological changes which indicate that a person is emotionally stimulated.

The polygraph can recognise only that some emotion has been aroused, not which one or why. Its supporters work on the assumption that the act of telling a lie involves more 'emotional arousal' than telling the truth. The results of most clinical tests on the accuracy of the polygraph machine are inconclusive at best, and downright critical at worst.

Another of Derren Brown's party pieces is to submit himself to a polygraph test – and beat it. He says the secret is to believe what you say. 'It is quite easy to respond to questions in a way which the machine will not recognise as deceptive behaviour.'

Successful use of the polygraph is entirely down to the ingenuity of the people operating the equipment and asking the questions. To be effective, the operator must 'prime the emotional pump' of the person being tested. If he is accused of theft, for example, and is asked if he stole the money, he might be able to deny it and control his emotions by justifying his action in his own mind as the redistribution of wealth, or as a victimless crime. However, if the questioner first invites the subject to agree that stealing is intrinsically wrong, and then asks specifically if he took the money from the safe *without asking permission*, it becomes emotionally much more difficult to tell what has now become a direct lie. The machine can then pick up on the increased emotional response.

The use of the polygraph in criminal cases in America demonstrates the strengths and weaknesses of the device.

During the 1996 Olympic Games in Atlanta, security guard Richard Jewell spotted a knapsack which turned out to contain a pipe bomb. He alerted police and helped move people away from the site before it exploded, killing one person and injuring more than 100 others. Three days later, a local newspaper announced: 'FBI Suspects Hero Guard May Have Planted Bomb'. Jewell had turned from hero to villain. To prove his innocence he agreed to take a polygraph test. After questioning Jewell for fifteen hours, the FBI came to the conclusion that he was telling the truth, and cleared him as a suspect. It was a good call. Another man was arrested several years later and admitted planting the bomb.

The limitations of the polygraph were evident from its use in the case of convicted murderer and rapist Roger Keith Coleman. Just hours before his scheduled execution back in May 1992, Coleman asked to be tested. He had always strenuously denied the charges against him. He took the test and failed it, and the execution went ahead as planned. But it was generally considered extremely doubtful that the operators of the polygraph machine were capable of making a distinction between the emotions that Coleman was feeling about his imminent execution and any anxiety he may have felt about lying.

Confusion between emotions aroused by lying and more innocent explanations is known in psychological circles as the

Othello Error. Othello assumed that Desdemona's agitation when accused of adultery was a sign of her guilt, and not her fear of being murdered by her enraged husband – a mistake anyone might make in the circumstances, and one which Othello would probably still have made even if he had been able to arrange for Desdemona to take the polygraph test.

* * *

Other lie-detecting technology is on its way. One invention promises to put an end to our habit of embellishing CVs with exaggerated qualifications, experience and previous salary details. You will recall the MORI poll which revealed that 25 per cent of Britain's working population misled their potential employer when applying for a job. An American firm, SAS, has developed a program called Text Miner which uses 'smart technology' to detect suspicious statements in CVs. It works by examining text patterns and number sequences for irregularities. It studies the language used to describe previous posts and checks whether it accurately reflects the job description. It can also check to see if academic institutions mentioned in a CV actually exist, and if they offer the courses claimed to have been taken. Text Miner can tap into an education database to ensure that candidates have not been lying about their academic records, and will also run checks on court records, bankruptcy and outstanding debts. Big Brother is watching your job application.

Meanwhile, in Britain, a team at Manchester Metropolitan University have come up with the 'Silent Talker', which electronically reads tiny facial micro-expressions and can, it's claimed, pinpoint eight out of ten liars in experimental conditions. This machine combines the skills of Derren Brown and Paul Ekman, all wrapped up in a laptop computer.

The suspect sits in front of a camera and is questioned while the computer analyses tiny movements of facial muscles, eyelids, eyebrows and the eyes themselves. Silent Talker registers mismatches and incongruities between micro-gestures – and sounds the alarm when a lie is detected. Dr Janet Rothwell, lead researcher on Silent Talker, says: 'The Yorkshire Ripper was interviewed at least five times before his lies were detected. I'd like to think that wouldn't happen with the Silent Talker around.'

And the Silent Talker would probably pick up on signals which appear to disprove my earlier assertion that liars cannot be identified by the length of their nose. Scientists at the University of Illinois have established that noses *do* get bigger when people lie. The very slight swelling occurs, they say, because when we lie our heart pumps faster and the sensitive nasal tissues swell up. This also accounts for the fact that people often touch or scratch their nose when they lie. Bill Clinton, apparently, touched his nose repeatedly while being questioned before a grand jury about his relationship with Monica Lewinsky.

A window on our lying souls

If Silent Talker can identify only eight out of ten lies, 20 per cent of lies would still go undetected, and those would probably be the most insidious lies, told by the most malevolent of liars. Perhaps the ultimate solution is to be found in the Sheffield laboratory of psychiatrist Sean Spence, who, as we've seen, uses an MRI scanner to identify and study the parts of our brain which 'light up' when we tell a lie. The areas of the brain specifically concerned with telling the truth have so far proved elusive.

'We've identified a small part of the jigsaw', says Dr Spence. But can he imagine his research ever being used by the police or courts to establish the truth in criminal cases? 'I can imagine the technology being used in high-stakes situations, probably in America first, in murder cases perhaps where life or death depended on the outcome, or to resolve a major miscarriage of justice.' He thinks it will take another five years before the technology is ready, but warns that there will still be major ethical issues to be resolved before it could be put into practice.

Meanwhile, scientists in America are not waiting for Dr Spence. A team at the University of Pennsylvania are developing the 'cognosensor', which beams infrared light through the skull into the brain. The pattern of reflected light indicates changes in blood flow. Its inventors explain that it works on the principle that when a person lies, more light is reflected, and the reflections radiate from a wider area than when the truth is being told.

And a new technique called 'brain fingerprinting' has already been used in a high-profile murder case in America. Jimmy Ray Slaughter was facing execution after being convicted of the brutal killing of his ex-girlfriend and their eleven-month-old child. Slaughter took the test in February 2004. He was asked questions while his brain activity was monitored via a series of electrodes placed around his scalp and connected to a standard EEG machine.

According to Dr Larry Farwell, the chief scientist behind brain fingerprinting, the test showed that, with a statistical confidence of 99.9 per cent, Slaughter did not have any memory of the details of the murder scene and therefore could not have been there at the time. On the basis of the test, Slaughter's lawyers filed an appeal.

Brain fingerprinting has been dismissed by scientists in Britain as fantasy, and the test on Jimmy Ray Slaughter failed to persuade the American judges, who rejected the appeal. Slaughter was executed by lethal injection on 17 March 2005.

The controversial technique has, nevertheless, been ruled as admissible in some American courts. Technology, psychology and now neurology are closing in on lies and the liars who tell them. Are we heading towards a distant future in which all lies, of black, white and intermediate hue, could be identified – a world in which lying had become impossible?

And what would that be like?

CHAPTER TEN

In defence of lies

Lies are necessary to life. That they should be so is part
and parcel of the terrible character of existence.

Nietzsche

I cannot deny it. I have told more than a few lies in my time. I'm
not proud of it, but there it is. The world kept turning. But does
it make me a bad person? Do *your* lies make *you* a bad person?
It depends, of course, on what kind of lies they are, and even if
they are actually lies at all. To consider this last point, we must
first take a brief excursion into Pedants' Corner.

The *Concise Oxford Dictionary* is suitably concise about
the meaning of the word 'lie'. In the opinion of its learned
compilers, a lie is 'an intentionally false statement'. Well, call
me picky, but that doesn't seem quite right. Should we accuse
William Shakespeare of lying when he declares 'All the world's
a stage', or David Beckham for announcing that he's 'over the
moon'? These are, after all, intentionally false statements.

Scholars who have pondered the whole business of lying
generally settle on a definition along the lines of 'communicating a falsehood with the intention to deceive', which seems
more like it.

In their subtle (and not so subtle) use of metaphor, both

Shakespeare and Beckham are, indeed, communicating false-hoods, but clearly neither intends to deceive. Rather, they are trying to accentuate the truth. Similarly, a schizophrenic who tells everyone he's Napoleon is clearly not telling the truth, but he's not lying, he's not trying to deceive. And a woman suffering from false memory syndrome, who wrongly claims to have been sexually abused in her childhood, isn't lying. Failure to tell the truth doesn't necessarily constitute a lie.

But are all lies bad? Certain lies, some of which we have already discussed, are not only acceptable but actually essential to the smooth running of our communal lives. Other lies, which we'll look at in a moment, are considered by some to be noble and justifiable. And we haven't yet touched on the fact that lies can also be entertaining, nor contemplated what life would be like without them.

Lying for pleasure

> Without lies humanity would perish of despair and boredom.
>
> Anatole France, novelist, satirist, playwright, poet

Life, if not actually 'nasty, brutish and short', certainly has its dull moments. For distraction we often turn to fiction. The phenomenal sales of J.K. Rowling's and Dan Brown's out-pourings suggest an insatiable desire for fantasy and escapism among children of all ages. Sales of novels massively outstrip those of non-fiction. Or we might seek comfort in the company of those loveable rogues in *EastEnders* or visit our local multi-plex, load up on popcorn and let that nice Mr Spielberg take us out of ourselves for an hour or two.

In all of these activities we are, in a sense, being lied to. They are imaginative, engaging lies, but lies nonetheless. Yes, these entertainments are clearly labelled as fiction, but they are 'untruths' and every effort is made by their tellers to get us to suspend our disbelief, to submit to the deception and accept it as truth. That seems to fulfil the definition of a lie. Certainly our emotional response – to laugh, to cry, to care – suggests that the deception has been accomplished.

We also lie to make ourselves more interesting to others. 'Yes, I'm a chartered accountant but I'm planning a single-handed voyage around the world in a bathtub. I just need to get the plumbing sorted out ...'

Phillip Kerr, in his introduction to the excellent *Penguin Book of Lies*, points out that you only have to imagine two dinner tables, one attended by the great men of truth, such as Augustine, Knox, Wesley, Kant, Hume and Bentham – and the other attended by such liars and tellers of tall stories as Machiavelli, Casanova, Rousseau, Napoleon, Oscar Wilde and Ernest Hemingway, to appreciate just how entertaining lying can be, especially when compared with the truth. At which dinner table would you prefer to sit?

And right on cue, a psychological study in the US reveals that teenage pupils who are the most convincing liars are often the most socially adept and popular among their classmates. The research done by the University of Massachusetts also concluded that girls lie more convincingly than boys.

Yes, lies can be enjoyable. Lies can make life more fun. And once a year, of course, we indulge in what is, essentially, a lie-fest.

On 1 April 1957 the television programme *Panorama* broadcast a short film about how an unusually mild winter had resulted in a bumper spaghetti harvest in southern Switzerland. The presenter was the hugely respected broadcaster Richard Dimbleby, the man who had brought the nation first-hand accounts of the D-Day landings. Now, over footage of a Swiss family pulling strands of pasta from a spaghetti tree and loading it into baskets, Dimbleby told viewers:

> The spaghetti harvest here in Switzerland is not, of course, carried out on anything like the tremendous scale of the Italian industry. Many of you, I'm sure, will have seen pictures of the vast spaghetti plantations in the Po valley. For the Swiss, however, it tends to be more of a family affair.

A delicious lie, which fooled many viewers, some of whom phoned the BBC to ask how they could grow their own spaghetti trees. A BBC spokesman told them to place a sprig of spaghetti in a tin of tomato sauce and hope for the best.

On 1 April 1977, *The Guardian* published a seven-page supplement to mark the tenth anniversary of San Serriffe, a small republic located in the Indian Ocean consisting of several semi-colon-shaped islands. Its two main islands, readers were informed, were named Upper Caisse and Lower Caisse. Its capital was Bodoni, and its leader was General Pica. *The Guardian* was inundated with calls from people wanting to know more. They hadn't noticed that everything about the islands was named after printers' terminology.

Taking delight in being lied to is not a peculiarly British phenomenon. On 1 April 1992 the US National Public Radio *Talk of the Nation* programme announced that Richard Nixon, unexpectedly, was running for President again. His new campaign slogan was 'I didn't do anything wrong, and I won't do it again'. Accompanying this announcement were audio clips of Nixon delivering his candidacy speech, performed by an actor.

Other great April Fool's jokes over the years have included the *Daily Mail*'s story about the Japanese long-distance runner Kimo Nakajimi who had entered the London Marathon but, on account of a translation error, thought that he had to run for 26 days, not 26 miles. Readers were encouraged to intercept him and warn him of his mistake. The great gullible public has also been taken in by stories of whistling carrots, Smell-o-vision, Big Ben going digital and Dutch Elm disease turning redheaded women into blondes. In 1997 an e-mail message was sent to millions of homes announcing that the internet would be shutting down for 24 hours for essential cleaning work.

I once attended a BBC Programme Review Board at which the spoof Radio 3 documentary *Blind Lemon Meringue – The one-armed Scottish blues bagpipe player* was to be discussed. At least a couple of the assembled senior BBC executives and programme-makers were labouring firmly under the illusion that Mr Meringue had actually existed.

All kinds of practical jokes are built upon lies and deception, though not everyone finds them amusing, of course. When working at a local radio station in Wales, some colleagues and I decided to play a not terribly sophisticated prank on local broadcaster Wynn Thomas, who came in once a week to record an epilogue. We left him a note saying that a vicar, the Reverend C. Lion, wanted to have a word with him about his next broadcast. We added the phone number of Bristol Zoo and recorded the ensuing conversation.

BRISTOL ZOO: Hello, Bristol Zoo.

WYNN: Hello, I'd like to speak to the Reverend C. Lion please.

BRISTOL ZOO (after a long pause): Yes sir. This is Bristol Zoo, we do have sea lions here.

WYNN: No, no. The *Reverend* C. Lion. I'm ringing from Swansea Sound. I do the epilogue.

BRISTOL ZOO: Someone is playing a joke on you, sir. This

> is Bristol Zoo. We have sea lions here, but no
> *Reverend* C. Lion.
> WYNN: No, no, no. You don't understand ...

And so on for several minutes. We found it hilarious, of course. Wynn simply couldn't understand that he was being fooled, that someone had lied to him. It did not compute. His reaction was born of the instinctive human need to believe that we are being told the truth. Even those who consider themselves to be particularly cynical and suspicious by nature might be surprised at how often they accept what they are told on trust.

My own doubting instincts were briefly overhauled the other morning when a man arrived at my front door claiming to have locked himself out of his house. He said he lived just along the street and needed to get a taxi to take his elderly father to hospital. I actually invited him into my house and offered him the phone, before it became clear (it was obvious, I know) that he didn't want to make a phone call, he wanted money. I told him I didn't have a penny in the house. We were both lying.

Our capacity to believe can lead us astray in many ways. Sometimes we totally lose sight of the distinction between fact and fiction. Producers of television and radio soaps, for example, are quite accustomed to receiving requests to attend the funerals of characters who have been 'killed off'.

On 16 January 1926, in the very early days of radio, the BBC transmitted an extraordinary programme called *Broadcasting the Barricades*. It began as an academic lecture, but was then interrupted by a series of 'from the scene' announcements that rioters were gathering in Trafalgar Square, the Savoy Hotel was ablaze, Big Ben blown up and a government minister hanged from a lamp-post. The reports, complete with sound effects, were enough to convince a public already worried about the threat of communism. There was considerable panic. One listener phoned the Admiralty, demanding that a warship be sent up the Thames to sort things out.

And twelve years later, even greater confusion ensued in America, when Orson Welles broadcast his famous production of *The War of the Worlds*.

> ... I'm speaking from the roof of Broadcasting Building, New York City. The bells you hear are ringing to warn the people to evacuate the city as the Martians approach. Estimated in the last two hours three million people have moved out along the roads to the north ... Hutchison River Parkway still kept open for motor traffic. Avoid bridges to Long Island ... hopelessly jammed. All communication with Jersey shore closed ten minutes ago. No more defenses. Our army is ... wiped out ... artillery, air force, everything wiped out. This may be the last broadcast. We'll stay here to the end ...

It was the evening of Sunday 30 October 1938. The CBS broadcast of the H.G. Wells classic was presented in the form of news bulletins and eye-witness accounts interrupting a music concert. As had happened with the BBC programme, many listeners failed to hear the opening announcements which made it clear it was a drama production. The *New York Times* reported the following day:

> A wave of mass hysteria seized thousands of radio listeners between 8.15 and 9.30 o'clock last night when a broadcast of a dramatization of H.G. Wells's fantasy, *The War of the Worlds*, led thousands to believe that an interplanetary conflict had started with invading

Martians spreading wide death and destruction in New Jersey and New York.

The broadcast disrupted households, interrupted religious services, created traffic jams and clogged communications systems ... at least a score of adults required medical treatment for shock and hysteria.

But even the newspaper reporting of the public reaction degenerated into fiction. Some papers reported the mass exodus of thousands of citizens, stampedes in theatres, heart attacks and even suicides. Almost all of it was complete nonsense, invented by newspaper proprietors who recognised a good story but who were also keen to discredit the new medium of radio which was muscling in on their territory.

Twinkle twinkle little lie

Astrology is another manifestation of our penchant for blurring the distinction between fact and fiction. In reality, most of the so-called astrologers who write newspaper and magazine columns wouldn't know their Uranus from their elbow. I don't want to shock anyone, but here's what's going on – they're making it up!

Some people allow their lives to be ruled by the alignment of the stars and the planets. Many more dismiss the whole business as rubbish, but will still check their stars every day, just in case. If it says today's a good day to make an investment, or to embark on a romantic adventure, maybe it is.

The simple truth – that no one, least of all ourselves, has any idea what the future has in store for us – is just too boring. We want our existence spiced up a little, and if that involves travelling into the realms of the not-entirely-factual, so be it. We extend this ambivalent attitude to the truth to a range of dubious things, like ghosts, ESP, scaly monsters living in the depths of Loch Ness, the *Daily Sport* – and magic.

Entertainer Ian Rowland specialises in 'mind magic and psychic-flavoured illusions'. In his stage act he draws on the techniques of the astrologer and tarot card reader and offers his audiences astounding insights into their lives. But, unlike most people in his business, he goes to great lengths to dispel any suggestion that he has supernatural powers.

> People are often amazed at what I can 'see' in the cards about their early life. What they don't realise is that I give the same account to everyone. We are all much less unusual than we think we are. For instance, most of us have had one serious accident or know someone who has. And many of us have had a relationship where distance was a problem, and so on.

He is, he says, no more psychic than a doormat. He just uses a bit of psychological trickery and relies on human nature – our instinct to believe.

Virtuous lies

If all lies involve deception, can they ever be justified or excused? St Augustine thought not. He categorised eight types of lies, in descending order of sinfulness – all absolutely forbidden by God. The worst lie was that 'uttered in the act of religious teaching', and the least serious was that 'which is harmful to no one and beneficial to the extent that it protects someone from physical defilement'. In all cases, however, the liar put his immortal soul at risk.

Other religious pronouncements are less proscriptive and allow liars a little more leeway. The Talmud, for example, permits Jews to tell lies to avoid appearing arrogantly know-ledgeable about religious matters, to avoid talking about marital relations and to avoid embarrassing one's host.

The 13th-century theologian Thomas Aquinas agreed with St Augustine that all lies are sins, but not that they are all mortal sins. He divided lies into three distinct categories: officious or helpful lies, intended to prevent someone from injury; jocose lies, told for pleasure or in jest; and malicious or mischievous lies, told to injure someone. It was only the third kind, the malicious lie, that Aquinas believed brought ever-lasting damnation of the soul.

So into which categories should we place our modern, 21st-century deceits and lies? Practical jokes and the entertaining lies found in literature and popular culture are clearly 'jocose' and therefore only moderately sinful. We obviously must put fraud and other criminal lies into the 'most serious' class and condemn their perpetrators to the fiery furnaces of hell. But where to put the falsehoods and dissemblings of advertising executives, politicians, journalists, estate agents and second-hand car salesmen, bearing in mind that we are all guilty of telling similar kinds of self-seeking lies? Must these too fall into the category of 'malicious or mischievous', consigning us all to hell? We definitely can't claim that they're funny.

But the other widely accepted get-out-of-hell ticket for the liar is for their deception to be classed as helpful or virtuous or noble. The trouble is that few can agree on a definition, and some, like Augustine, won't have any of it.

Would, for example, a lie told to win a battle, to save lives by ending a war, be virtuous? Were the Allies justified in deceiv-ing the Germans by transmitting false signals about the proposed sites for the D-Day landings? I suppose it depends on which side you're fighting for, or, from a non-combatant's perspective, on whose side you suppose God or righteousness to be.

Excluding lies told to entertain, which clearly fall into a category of their own, can any deceptions ever be entirely justifiable or good? Is there such a thing as a lie that harms no one, or can even the whitest of lies seem black from another's perspective?

What about the doctor who lies to a seriously ill patient about his condition, to spare him unnecessary anxiety? Is it preferable to telling him bluntly: 'It's terminal – don't start reading any long books'? The intended kindness of the former approach may backfire if the patient, when he eventually learns the truth, feels angry and betrayed, having lost the opportunity to make the most of his remaining time (or indeed to finish *War and Peace*).

British navy Commander Ian Riches headed a team which in August 2005 spent three days fighting to free a stricken Russian mini-submarine entangled in fishing nets on the floor of the Pacific Ocean. As they worked to slice through the nets, Commander Riches told the world's press that he was 'confident' that the seven Russian crewmen could be saved, even though their oxygen supply was rapidly running out. Later, during emotional scenes following the successful rescue, he admitted: 'I was lying.' But, in trying to spare the Russian crew's relatives unnecessary anguish, he had run the risk of offering them false hope.

Krishna advises Hindus that 'by telling a lie to save a life, one is not touched by sin'. So let's say some sort of villain arrives at your door and threatens to kill your friend who is hiding there. To lie to the would-be murderer would seem reasonable in the circumstances, but 18th-century philosopher Immanuel Kant argued that to do so would be morally wrong.

Kant believed that to lie is 'a crime of man against his own person and a baseness which must make a man contemptible in his own eyes.' To be truthful, he said, is 'a sacred and absolutely commanding decree of reason, limited by no expediency.'

Kant, with a clear conscience presumably, would tell his friend's would-be assassin: 'He's hiding in a cupboard in the front bedroom.' Which would be tough on his friend, unless, I suppose, he shared the same absolutist philosophical attitude.

Moving into less extreme territory, the psychologist Paul Ekman offers some ground rules for prospective lie-tellers who don't want to end up in hell. He suggests they put themselves in the position of the person they are about to lie to. Would they feel betrayed or hurt or exploited, or would they understand? Some years back, Professor Ekman underwent tests for cancer but decided not to tell his wife about them. 'My wife said she thought I seemed worried about something. I said I wasn't, that everything was fine. That was a serious lie. But why should I make her worry? When she found out, she didn't feel betrayed, she understood my motive – although she would have preferred that I had told her the truth.'

But he says the well-intentioned liar treads a slippery slope: 'He might have an affair, or a one-night stand and tell himself that his wife really wouldn't want to know about it. Is he sure, or is he simply trying to have his cake and eat it too? You must put yourself in the position of the other person. Would they really want to be lied to in the circumstances?'

Ekman adds that, in the case of lying about an affair, the cost of lying can be the destruction of trust. And no one knows how to re-establish trust. Many relationships end, not because of the offence, but because of the lie about the offence. 'It is hard to live with someone you can't trust', he says.

Parental lies, as we have discussed earlier, are not without their consequences. We lie to our children on a very regular basis – about Father Christmas and tooth-fairies, that an injection won't hurt, that broccoli is delicious or that we are 'nearly there'. The worry is that these gentle and well-intentioned lies set an example – that the truth is some sort of option, to be adopted or discarded as convenient. The signals can be very confusing: 'You mustn't lie, darling, or teddy won't be your friend.'

And under what circumstances could it be argued that a political lie was acceptable or even virtuous? Plato argued that a 'noble lie' was one told to the people in order to safeguard social harmony. But what if, entirely hypothetically speaking, a British Prime Minister, in order to justify taking the nation to war, were to exaggerate the potential danger posed by a Middle East country, by claiming, let's say, that the dictator running the country was capable of launching weapons of mass destruction within 45 minutes? That Prime Minister might believe that a greater good was served by this small deception – that Western commercial interests in that country might be re-established and, more altruistically, that democracy might be returned to a subjugated people. Would that be OK? The 2005 General Election result suggests that, by and large, the public thinks it would.

A world without lies

The progress being made by scientists in identifying the parts of the brain engaged in the process of lying raises the prospect of a very intriguing future. What would happen if genetic engineering enabled us to suppress our lying grey matter, leaving us incapable of deception? Deceit, euphemism, exaggeration, obfuscation, falsehoods and outright lies – all gone. What would that be like?

For a start, the legal system would be redundant; no judge or jury would be needed to determine guilt or innocence. We would all go quietly to the station. Indeed, much crime would no longer be possible. 'Who will give me a fiver for this bottle of coloured water with a Chanel No 5 label on it?' Or: 'Dear Sir, I am a Nigerian email fraudster and was just wondering if you would like to deposit a considerable amount of money into my bank account for no particular reason.'

What other benefits might accrue? Estate agents would all have to follow the disarmingly honest approach pioneered by the Roy Brooks agency, along the lines of: 'A deeply unattractive property suitable for gullible couple with more money than sense'. Promotion of fast food would be reduced to the one word which truly describes it – 'fast'.

But there would be a considerable downside. We would lose all the entertainment and fun associated with lies and deception. A world without literature, drama, comedy and practical jokes doesn't really sound very attractive. How dull it would be if we had to make do with plain old reality. You only have to watch reality TV to know that this is true.

And what would be the consequence of losing all those valuable, but intrinsically deceitful tools of social interaction: the euphemistic lies told every day to deal with embarrassing or difficult situations, the ego-massaging flattery and affirmation by which we provide one another with 'unconditional positive regard'? Without this lubricating oil, society would become abrasive and fractious.

We would see copious amounts of what psychiatrist Willard Gaylin has described as 'truth dumping' – the unnecessary dispensing of honesty without concern for the damage it might do. Parents would be unstinting in their frankness about their offspring's inadequacies. A three-year-old's picture of mummy would be dismissed as 'unconvincing', a rendition of 'Three Blind Mice' as 'tuneless.' Cruel perhaps, but we might be spared the more execrable *X-Factor* contestants. Doctors would bluntly present the full, gory details of the pain and suffering involved in a procedure and the unlikelihood of a full and speedy recovery. Wedding vows would need to be rethought, with the words 'I might' replacing 'I do'. Husbands and wives, no longer able to conceal their infidelities, would spend their evenings being honest about each other's annoying habits. Extra-marital sex would not, I think, be replaced by *extra* marital sex.

Paul Ekman sees such a future as peopled with fully functioning adults – colleagues, lovers – all with the 'emotional control and disguise of a three-month-old infant'. It's not a world that he would wish to be part of.

A world without lies would almost certainly be a nightmare. It's possible that we would either stop talking to each other altogether or lead our lives in a permanent state of confrontation. In the view of psychologist Darius Galasinski: 'A world without lies would be too cruel. You would have to admit to your hostess that you hated the soup.'

Or as Oscar Wilde has it: 'Telling the truth makes one very unpopular at the club.'

Lie a little less each day

Having spent much of the last nine chapters warning of the dangers lurking in the evil jungle of lies surrounding us, I fear I may now have given the impression that lies are a jolly good thing and truth a dull and tiresome inconvenience. Turn back and start again if you're inclined towards that conclusion.

There's no way to say for sure if lying is actually on the increase. But it certainly seems to be. What is absolutely clear is that there's too much of it about – particularly the cruel, manipulative and self-seeking variety. As a species we have come to behave as if we are no longer satisfied with the truth, finding it inconvenient and limiting. We take the lies of politicians, businessmen, journalists and the rest for granted, and are no longer surprised when they are exposed. Indeed, they encourage us to believe that lying is acceptable. We lie because we think everyone else is doing it, and fear that we will disadvantage ourselves if we tell the truth. It's a vicious circle of deceit. The individual who at least attempts to get through life by being scrupulously honest and trusting is invariably seen (and indeed treated) as a fool.

We tell lies because we can. Our ability to tell lies, psychologist Martin Skinner told us, is part of being human. There are advantages to being intelligent, sophisticated beings, but our capacity to lie is not necessarily one of them.

We might become slightly nicer people if we were to pick and choose the lies we tell a little more carefully. If the average person currently tells five or six lies a day, let's try to cut it down to three or four – and make most of them of the kind or entertaining variety.

Despite the reservations just expressed about a world without lies, maybe we should try having a National Tell the Truth Day – just to see what happens. We might learn some useful, or at least interesting, things about each other. We would surely gain some insight into our lying nature – that is, if we made it through the exercise alive.

Or maybe you should just go it alone. Unilaterally declare yourself a lie-exclusion zone. Go ahead, try it in your home or workplace. Tell everybody exactly what you think. Say precisely what you mean. But if it gets you into trouble, don't try blaming me for suggesting it.

I'll say you're lying.

Sources

Scott Adams, *Dilbert and the Way of the Weasel*, Boxtree, 2003

Scott Adams, *The Dilbert Principle*, HarperCollins, Boxtree, 1997

J.A. Barnes, *A Pack of Lies*, Cambridge University Press, 1994

Sissella Bok, *Lying*, Vintage, 1989

Paul Ekman, *Telling Lies*, W.W. Norton, 2001

D.J. Enright (ed.), *Fair of Speech: The Uses of Euphemism*, Oxford University Press, 1985

Harry G. Frankfurt, *On Bullshit*, Princeton University Press, 2005

Darius Galasinski, *The Language of Deception*, Sage, 2000

Carl Hausman, *Lies We Live By*, Routledge, 2000

Bill Hicks, *Love All The People*, Constable, 2004

John Humphrys, *Lost for Words*, Hodder and Stoughton, 2004

Luke Harding, David Leigh and David Pallister, *The Liar: The Fall of Jonathan Aitken*, Penguin, 1997

Philip Kerr (ed.), *The Penguin Book of Lies*, Penguin, 1990

Judith S. Neaman and Carole G. Silver, *The Wordsworth Book of Euphemism*, Wordsworth, 1995

Matthew Parris, *Scorn*, Hamish Hamilton, 1994

Samuel Pepys, *The Diary of Samuel Pepys*, Random House, 2003

Steven Pinker, *The Language Instinct*, Penguin, 1994

Private Eye, Ian Hislop (ed.), 2005

Leigh Rutledge, *The World's Greatest Lies*, Michael O'Mara, 1999

Evelin Sullivan, *The Concise Book of Lying*, Picador, 2001

Malcolm Turnbull, *Spycatcher*, Heinemann, 1988

Penny Vincenzi, *The Compleat Liar*, Cassell, 1979

Aldert Vrij, *Detecting Lies and Deceit*, Wiley, 2000

Don Watson, *Gobbledygook*, Atlantic, 2004

Jamie Whyte, *Bad Thoughts: A Guide to Clear Thinking*, Corvo, 2003

The Wit and Wisdom of Oscar Wilde, Crown, 1999